THE
Modern Garden Makers

THE
Modern Garden Makers

SALLY COURT

FOREWORD BY

John Brookes

WARD
LOCK

First published in the United Kingdom in 1999 by Ward Lock

Designed and produced by
Cardinal Publishing Limited
59 Twyford Avenue
London N2 9NR

Distributed in the United States of America by Sterling Publishing Co. Inc.
387 Park Avenue South, New York, NY 10016-8810

A CIP catalogue record for this book is available from the British Library.

ISBN 0-304-35325-6

Design Director: Pedro Prá-Lopez
Editor: Tamar Karet
Design and page formatting: Frances Prá-Lopez
Plant list and Index: Margaret Crowther
Colour reprographics: Inka Graphics Limited, Cardiff
Printing and binding: L.E.G.O. SpA, Vicenza

Ward Lock
Illustrated Division
The Orion Publishing Group
Wellington House
125 Strand
London WC2R 0BB

Page 1 photograph: Ian Smith, Acres Wild; *garden design:* Acres Wild
Page 2 photograph: J. S. Sira, Garden Picture Library; *garden design:* Dan Pearson

Contents

Majestic verbascums at Denmans

Foreword

JOHN BROOKES

Since the end of the Second World War there has been a remarkable change in many aspects of life and none more so than in the garden. I think that the garden designer's clientele has changed, the small garden has come upon us, and the advent of the television garden has brought an interest in the subject of design very much to the forefront. The content of this book shows a huge range of styles from the environmentalist to the artist, but underpinning them all is that sense of design, a feeling for mass and space, and a facility for the inner eye to project the plan into some future time. For garden art is one of the few that has this added fourth dimension.

Sally Court has presented us with a sumptuous book the breadth of which I believe one would find in no other country's garden design output. And this, of course, is to do with our rich inheritance of garden makers. If she has not influenced us directly, discussion instigated by Miss Jekyll's theories most certainly has. I'm not old enough to remember her, but Brenda Colvin, for whom I first worked as a student, had met her. As a student myself, I did my dissertation on the Festival Gardens at Battersea, and met Russell Page to discuss them. I remember the visits and lectures of Roberto Burle Marx, and later had discussions with an old Percy Cane at the Chelsea Flower Show. Lanning Roper, Peter Coates and Susan Jellico were all plants people I knew in this rich tradition of plantsmanship, which is the emphasis on which the book rests. Christopher Lloyd, Beth Chatto, Rosemary Verey and Penelope Hobhouse continue to provide this bridge and link with the Modern Garden Makers who sometimes, adding a greater design dimension, extend the scope and scale of garden design work into the future.

At the end of the millennium, this books makes its timely statement and provides a worthy stepping stone along the way.

John Brookes

CHAIRMAN, SOCIETY OF GARDEN DESIGNERS
CLOCK HOUSE, DENMANS, JUNE 1999

Introduction

SALLY COURT

What exactly is modern garden design? Where is it coming from? The debate continues, and constantly causes tempers to flare. Is there a standard to follow? Who is right? Should we throw all the old traditions away and move towards modernism? The designers in this book represent a number of views. This is the very dynamic of the garden; it is always evolving, allowing for experimentation and change. Without this diverse thinking we would all be left with hybrid tea roses, rockeries filled with small conifers or the ubiquitous leylandii hedge so beloved in the 1950s.

Although garden design has been part of landscape history since time immemorial, it is only in recent years that it has become recognized as an art form. There is a huge diversity of imaginative approaches which designers bring to landscaping. Some of these are instantly recognizable as links to the past, while others clearly look to the future for inspiration. Many private commissions have become the canvases for the garden and landscape designer to transform the mundane into the really spectacular.

Traditionally gardens have been seen as oases of calm and tranquillity, havens where the senses are teased into a response. They have been used to illustrate the status of both the owner and the place. Whether formal lawns or intimate informal courtyards, grand entrances or settings to display works of art, gardens have always been the perfect foil.

Every garden designer has a different approach to a project. Each has a unique way of working to find the right excitement to generate the perfect solution to the design brief. Each and every one of them is idiosyncratic. All are able to visualize the end result on the grand scale, as well as inspire the contractors to interpret their schemes off paper and onto the land.

Nearly all of the really brilliant designers work to a discipline and rarely wander off the main plan. They will amend and modify, but the 'skeleton' remains intact. Certain shapes repeat themselves; clipped box balls are reflected in the shape of topiary bay trees or domes made by the natural habit of another plant. Great architectural spikes of phormiums are shadowed by the smaller iris leaves and yet more delicate ornamental grasses. Or colour will been seen dotted among planting schemes throughout the garden, such as the yellow of the *Hemerocallis* 'Stella d'Oro' seen again in the *Coreopsis verticillata* 'Grandiflora', creating a natural rhythm, like waves through the garden. Rhythms are introduced to create a harmonious entity, to evoke moods within a blank space.

Each of the designers featured in this book comes from a different background. Although their styles are diverse, inspiration for their creations often derives from the same source, a factor which spurs them into making the site come alive. It is an affinity with the surroundings and it comes from the soul. This is what is meant by a 'sense of place'. Each interpretation will show the special talents of the designer, and the end result will reflect the passion generated by this very focussed group.

We are becoming more and more environmentally aware and ecology plays an increasing role in the way in which we interpret a design. Rather than imposing a garden design on the landscape without a thought as to how it relates to the greater horizon, our ability to link it with the environs is now paramount.

This volume includes an eclectic collection taken from the many and diverse British designers who are currently practising around the world. These few are some of the most inspirational, the ones other designers seek to emulate. Of the fourteen included here, it is interesting to note that five are qualified landscape architects and one an architect, two are sculptors, and three trained in horticulture before entering garden design. The remaining three also had a previous career, though less obviously related to the art of gardens, namely graphic design, sport and fine art, and I myself first had a career in marketing and advertising. The one thing that links us all is our vision of connecting our creativity with the greater landscape.

John Brookes was the first British designer to lead us into a new way of thinking about our gardens. His books and teachings have been very influential in encouraging us towards simplicity in design and a more natural use of plants. Sarah Eberle, Debbie Roberts and Ian Smith have all chosen to follow an ecological route with their very naturalistic designs which blend the new into the existing scenery. With his keen sense of place and understanding of different world philosophies, Dan Pearson has helped us to look more thoroughly at the plants we use. Julie Toll also has an innate understanding of our environment, but where so many of us will use cultivated plants she has painstakingly studied our wild flora and uses it to create the most evocative wild flower meadows.

Our imaginations have been stretched fully by the work of Paul Cooper, Bonita Bulaitis, Cleve West and Johnny Woodford. Their reasoning is very different, but each of their gardens is electrically charged and arouses even the most jaded critic into a response. The clean architectural lines of minimalist designers like Christopher Bradley-Hole and Andrew Wilson are very far removed from our traditional gardens. It is refreshing to see how their work highlights the beauty of a single plant, and leads us to begin to appreciate how, all on its own, the colour green can engender a sense of calm. The big, bold architectural planting found in Anthony Paul's work is equally stimulating, providing such wonderful textural patterns and interactions with light. This is a style with which I find myself particularly in sympathy.

I have been incredibly lucky to have met all these designers and been able to follow their careers over the past few years. Whether it has been at garden shows or through the media and seminars, each has opened my eyes to the development of modern garden design. I have worked alongside several as a Council Member of the Society of Garden Designers, and this has allowed me a very personal insight into their motivation and enthusiasm for promoting outstanding design.

British designers are often criticized by their overseas contemporaries for being stuck in the past, but this is by no means fair. We have the most tremendous garden heritage in the UK and it is only natural that we should use it, modify it and update it, but we are not so inward-looking that we cannot learn from our contemporaries abroad. Their influence on the way we design is very much in evidence in our gardens. The names of Wolfgang Oehme, James van Sweden, Piet Ouldolf, Tadao Ando, Roberto Burle Marx, Isabelle Greene and Tofher Delaney keep recurring in our conversations.

Controversy reigns within the whole of the garden design community as to what should be included in our plans. At a recent *Gardens Illustrated* seminar, Anna Pavord questioned whether we were right to dismiss traditional plants from today's garden design. Surely there is still a place for a rose in the right setting? Personally I still use roses and so does Dan Pearson. I am sure I remember Tofher Delaney berating an audience of

British garden designers, saying that Gertrude Jekyll is dead. It is true I see no signs of her mammoth borders in this book, but her colour theory is still very relevant.

In Britain, we have a reputation for living on past glories and this may be true to a certain extent. We have to remember that much of our architecture dates back a long way and many of our new buildings still reflect these roots. Land is at a premium and our housing stock sits cheek by jowl on little plots with a view of our neighbour's back garden. To make matters worse, new developments spring up all over the countryside, but very few really stir the spirit. And, in general, the owners seem quite happy with their lot.

Occasionally an architect will surprise us with something outstandingly different or shockingly contentious. Someone like Daniel Liebeskind, the renowned, ground-breaking architect who has aroused the most fervent objections to his design for the extension to the Victoria and Albert Museum in London. Only when the public accepts artists like him will we be allowed to have our heads.

Happily, there is a strong undercurrent of modernism emerging in our designs. One particular complaint that has been raised by John Brookes and echoed by others is that it is only people outside the UK who ask for modern schemes. However, clients are gradually being educated into a new way of thinking about their gardens in terms of both the hard landscaping and the planting.

To make our gardens come alive, it is up to garden designers to have the courage of our convictions. We need to be able to persuade the public that contemporary designs in their many guises are as aesthetically pleasing as the gardens of a previous era. Clients who have faith and trust in their designers to come up with the right solution will always get the best results. Gradually this new contemporary movement is gaining momentum. Garden design is a wonderfully rewarding process. The incredibly varied and stimulating gardens we see around us, many of which are displayed in the pages of this book, are our reward.

CHAPTER ONE

Origins

The doyen of contemporary
British garden design

JOHN BROOKES

ABOVE & BELOW: *A raised terrace allows for superb views over the countryside. The natural landscaping blends in with the fields and hills beyond.*

In the early 1970s everyone was talking about a garden designer with a completely fresh approach. With his book *Outside Room* published in 1969, John Brookes opened up a completely new way of looking at just what a garden is. Soon his clean architectural lines, uncluttered corners, bold planting shapes and bright colours took hold. However, John admits it is still an uphill battle to convince clients to do away with fussy, busy planting schemes. "I am only asked to carry out contemporary designs by my overseas clients, with just a few exceptions here in Britain." Other garden designers echo this. John's bold geometric style is very disciplined; there are no unnecessary embellishments to his work. Pure architectural lines, simplicity and repeated blocks of colour are the key. He always links his concepts to the surroundings; they contrast with it, but are always complementary.

With this timber-clad house on a rise overlooking a wetland, John has introduced timber decking and stone terraces at different levels. Where better to view the natural-looking, man-made pond? Linear brick retaining walls provide deep platforms for planting which are filled with subtle shades of blue, grey, silver and yellow. The tall, graceful *Stipa gigantea* provides a fountain of seed heads. The severe lines of the walls are softened by the plant textures and the delicate colour combinations. An oversized white stone ball finial is the only man-made decoration.

LEFT: *Native sedges and bulrushes make a fine autumn and winter display at the edge of this natural-looking pool in the meadow.*

When John first came to the Clock House at Denmans the garden belonged to a passionate plantswoman, Mrs Joyce Robinson. It was and still is open to the public. Over the years he oversaw the garden work, gradually stamping it with his own character. John now owns Denmans and runs both his renowned garden design school and his design practice from the Clock House.

Many of John's trademarks can be seen here. His love of structure is uncompromising, whether in the form of a pivotal evergreen shrub, hard landscaping or water. The colours of leaves, flowers and stems are lovingly considered and plants positioned so that they blend to catch the sunlight or reflect the sky. Colour themes recur throughout to allow the eye to rest and the mind to grasp the whole picture. The golden yew in the herb garden echoes the tones of the great euphorbias so beloved by John, and the bitter lime greens of ladies mantle, *Alchemilla mollis*, and feverfew leaves. The herb garden is protected by old high brick walls which create a warm and sheltered microclimate. Herbs are grown through gravel bisected by natural stone paths, allowing them to spread and mingle. Happy self-seeding makes for a joyful mix which is helped by the judicious weeding out of rogues.

RIGHT: *A bright blue Lutyens bench sits in sharp contrast to the golden yelllow and white of the surrounding plants.*

LEFT: *A multitude of herbs grown through a gravel mulch mix together to form a vibrant mat of colour. Many varieties of low-spreading thyme grow through the paving to complement the taller herbs and herbaceous perennials. Orange-petalled Iceland poppies and yellow verbascum have happily self-seeded among the herbs.*

Strong planting statements are an essential part of John's philosophy, whether he is using one plant in extensive blocks to provide continuity or featuring one huge species on its own as a show stopper. Experimentation and the environment are two of his bywords. Working with the landscape rather than trying to impose upon it makes for a more natural garden.

In his water gardens John uses plants to enhance an area and make it more intriguing. Actually, one of these has no water at all. Instead it resembles a dry stream bed, a device which allows the use of drought-loving plants. The 'stream', created from sweeps of gravel, follows the existing contours through the garden as it runs down to meet a natural pond. The gravel bed itself allows many of John's favourite plants to flourish and self-seed. They are planted up in random clumps and singletons, with little or no intermingling. The gravel mulch prevents them rotting off over winter and provides a perfect contrast to the planting style around the pool.

And what a contrast. The dry stream bed is in a very hot, dry area while the pool is much more shaded and has a completely different ambience. A dense thicket of plants creates a verdancy not found elsewhere in the garden. Though it gives the impression of being wild, it has been planted up with great care to provide colour and textural interest throughout the seasons. Gravel slowly grades into larger knapped flints and cobbles until it becomes a graded beach leading down to the pool. A statue of a boy is placed at the edge so that he disappears into the planting backdrop. The elegant tiered *Viburnum plicatum* and the dominant giant hogweed (*Heracleum sphondylium*) are clustered high above.

A great swathe of *Caltha palustris*, the long-lost kingcup of river and stream banks, lies at the margins of the water and provides a banner of bright golden yellow in springtime. Later in the season the planting will become even more dense. The pool is hidden by a mass of water-lily leaves, and spots of sunlight touch the spires of yellow-flowering ligularia and brighten the thick canopy of leaves.

LEFT: *A carefully placed statue of a seated boy, by Marion Smith, looks out over the shaded pool.*

ABOVE: *The pool is covered by lily pads which reflect the sunlight. Giant hogweed* (Heracleum sphondylium) *and* Ligularia *'The Rocket' make a spectacular foliar backdrop.*

BELOW: *The garden is no less impressive in winter when the blazing stem colours of dogwoods* (Cornus alba *and* C. stolonifera) *light up a chill morning.*

Mrs Robinson first started to work with plants in a more naturalistic way and introduced gravel beds to Denmans. John has reduced the grassed areas to a minimum. Experimental planting with native and introduced species has been very successful, allowing for a wilder style. Unrestrained by rigid borders, they seem to drift through the sweeps of gravel. The light filters through to groups of low evergreens. Other shrubs that thrive naturally at the edge of a woodland have also been planted under the tree canopy, for further diversification as well as glorious autumn colour. At the edge of the canopy verbascums have been seeded into the gravel.

Elsewhere the wild look has been cultivated. Instead of the sparseness under the trees, lush plantings of perennials have been encouraged to blend in to create a contemporary canvas of muted colours. There is nothing harsh to jar the spirits, just a harmonious whole. Soft textures from fennel, lilies and arching grasses, in silver, grey and tones of green blend with the complementary yellow of the achillea flowers and *Alchemilla mollis*.

LEFT: *Harmonious lilac pink from a small-leafed syringa, the flowers of comfrey and purple-leafed sage contrast with the silver grey of the ice-plant (sedum) and verbascum.*

RIGHT: *Once the bulbs and wild flowers have died down, the meadow is mown once a month to keep it under control.*

BELOW: *Deep purple and cream lupins, grouped together with chives, green and purple sages and fennels, foxgloves and pink flowering roses, create a muted and rather masculine combination.*

In this absorbing garden there are cool colours to soothe, warmer shades to stir the emotions, and the occasional shock to wake up jaded senses. Plants have to work for their space in the overall plan. Favourite plants are repeated to provide a natural rhythm, but every now and then a particularly intimate combination stops you in your tracks. The spring-flowering lilac (syringa) with its mauve flowers and the pink bells of the comfrey nestle into the dark purple-leafed sage, offset by the large velvety glaucous leaves of a verbascum. The herb garden with its medley of mauves and strong verticals reflects this haze of pastels, while the dark purple lupins in front of the cream ones appear to emerge from a sea of soft blue created by the nepeta.

John's treatment of the grass is also unconventional. In spring, areas are left to allow wild flowers and bulbs to meld into a meadow. His use of bulbs and other cultivated perennials makes a most interesting mix within the tall grasses, creating a wild flower meadow with a twist. Mown paths run through the meadow, allowing a contrast in textures.

LEFT: *A cruciform lily pool, planted with acquatic plants, provides a serene focus to the brick-paved courtyard.*

BELOW: *One of John's hallmarks is to allow self-seeded plants to spread through gravel to bring about a wild feel to a garden.*

A strong bond often develops between garden designers and their clients and John is frequently asked to design more than one garden for a client. When a style suits the location and an easy working relationship develops, it can be continued from site to site. The first garden that John created for Mr and Mrs Holland in Sussex had a sense of intimacy. A formal cross-shaped lily tank was set into a clay brick terrace. It gives the impression of being enclosed and protected on all sides by the house and is planted in a style reminiscent of ancient Islamic Paradise Gardens.

We all draw on our knowledge of architectural and garden history, and John spent a considerable period of time teaching in Iran. Here the geometric aspect of the water feature, the cross, the herringbone pattern of the brick paviors and square planting pockets follow his principles of strong structure and simplicity. The plants are chosen to blur the hard edges without losing the underlying design. Spouts are concealed at the corners of the pool, allowing jets of water to arc into the centre of the lily pond creating a perfectly balanced symmetry. At one end of the lily tank a bench positioned in a sheltered spot provides a perfect place to enjoy the tranquility of the garden.

RIGHT: *The formal simplicity of topiary brings an elegance to an old manor house. Water tanks set on two levels link the upper and lower terraces.*

BELOW RIGHT: *Box and yew clipped with precision provide a foil to the perennial planting, while informal planting round the door introduces a welcoming note.*

The Hollands' next garden at a dignified old manor house required quite different treatment. Here John began by working with existing features and extracting the essence of the past without copying it. Huge yews clipped into remarkable shapes could overwhelm less considered planting in the parterre garden. Bright green regimented box edges the borders to continue the formal framework. And here is the contrast: light and airy planting fills the centres. An ostensibly random selection of herbaceous plants, evocative of period style, produces an exuberant patchwork of colour, and introduces a touch of levity against the formidable backdrop.

Elegant water channels are fundamental to John's plans. In this garden the top terrace is linked to the one below by two large, mirror-clear oblong pools which reflect the scudding clouds. Understated lead spouts let into the retaining wall provide the smallest of water movement. Square stepping stones just break the surface of the pools to allow access. Planting is kept to a minimum on the house terrace. Clipped box is used to hide the top of the retaining wall from the house. This sets the scene for the massive rose garden at the lower level.

LEFT: *This aerial view of the English Garden at Barakura shows the formal garden with its central statue and rose arbours. In the distance a pathway meanders through the lawns.*

BELOW: *A series of stone pillars hold up the wooden crossbeams that support the pink rambling roses. Benches offer a place to view the gardens beyond.*

Designers are frequently asked to travel across continents to develop a scheme in some far-flung corner. This generates a cross-fertilization of ideas which leads to a merging of styles and innovative solutions. Heated debates range as to whether one theory or practice is right for one country and should not be imposed on another. Purists believe that only native plants should be used, while others feel that the environment is the major concern. Many believe that experimentation is the way forward. Designers like John believe that plant material must be suited to local conditions even if it is not native to the country.

Many of John's commissions take him abroad. Familiarization with the local environment and social requirements and an assessment of the native flora and fauna is essential before undertaking such a project. He believes that no matter where you are located a usable terraced area should be adjacent to the house or within the hub of the garden. By its very nature, a terraced area has to be a formal structure, and this in turn allows for a less rigid approach to the remainder of the site. The same is true for a garden open to the public, and this is how he approached the planning of the English Garden at Barakura in Japan. Land is at a premium in Japan, so any that is accessible to the public must be designed with great care. The Japanese psyche is steeped in Zen teaching so it would be inappropriate for a foreign designer to try to impose a cottage-style garden on their landscape.

LEFT: *A narrow lily pond runs along the base of the beautifully crafted stone wall. The visitors' terrace looks out across the garden.*

Nevertheless, John's brief was to design an English-style garden and that is what he has accomplished.

John has designed a series of gardens built into the side of a hill on different levels and linked by a serpentine path. The result is one of tranquil beauty, with swathes of green and dense tree planting. John has not compromised his design principles. Simplicity is of the very essence, for good structure is what holds superb design together. Here his genius lies in how he has managed to bring in Japanese artistry in an appropriate way.

The formal areas are built to linear designs, each locking into the next. A magnificent stone wall retains the visitors' terrace, but this is no ordinary wall. Using large chunks of roughly hewn stone, it incorporates a random pattern within a strict stratum of narrow horizontal pieces. At the base of the wall an oblong lily pool runs along its entire length. In another area, a gravel garden with plants tumbling onto the path is concealed from immediate view. Elegantly proportioned stone pillars supported by solid wooden cross beams and smothered by roses shelter seats that look out over the garden. This border, filled with John's favourite blend of colour, is redolent of Denmans' borders. The meadow conjures up images of wild flowers, but if you look closely you will see the tall heads of golden-yellow daylilies (hemerocallis), and blue iris flowers scattered through the grass.

ABOVE: *John has created a 'wild flower meadow' by introducing hardy perennials, blue-flowered iris and yellow hemerocallis into the grass which will continue flowering year on year.*

John was the obvious choice when the Chicago Botanic Garden sought a designer to implement a new feature. Here was the leading British garden designer, trained by the late Sylvia Crowe, with an awe-inspiring track record. With numerous books to his name, a garden design school, and an international lecture circuit as well as a garden open to the public, he would surely give the Botanic Garden a truly English garden.

This was a virgin site with no constraints. Helped by changes in level, John divided the site into a series of rooms, ranging from a cottage garden to a garden at a lower level set round a sunken pool. This is no reproduction of Sissinghurst. John pays homage to Vita Sackville-West and the English gardening traditions, but he does not copy them. Sharp lines and contemporary materials

Giant checkerboards created from clipped box hedging and Salvia nemorosa, *'East Friesland', provide contrast on either side of the pool.*

bring the garden up-to-date, and the use of larger than life proportions makes it quite breathtaking. With a huge open sky, John has used the light to add a further dimension to the setting. As with all his designs, the garden is based on rectilinearity. There are no unnecessary curves added to the borders. Instead, carefully chosen plants cascade over firm lines, while traditional plants are used in a contemporary manner.

John's considered choice of hard landscaping materials is paramount to the success of the garden. The mellow red bricks used in building the walls add warmth to the pale tones of stone balustrading, columns, gravel and an oversized ball finial. An imposing pergola leads the eye to one of his concessions to the past, a Lutyens bench set under a wall plaque. The planting is certainly from a different time. Huge alternate squares of clipped box and the *Salvia nemorosa*, 'East Friesland', form a giant checkerboard on either side of the raised circular pool. This is the only round feature in the entire garden. Its stark simplicity, featuring only an unadorned fountain, proves that less is more.

Light can change the mood of a garden, and the colours of plants play an important role. In the formal garden, John has chosen a single flower shape, the daisy in all its forms and sizes, in deep pinks and dark yellows. When the sun catches them, they take on an intrinsic jewel-like quality of their own. This is one of John's few richly-coloured planting schemes. Equally successful is his plant combination of *Rosmarinus officinalis* 'Miss Jessopp's Upright' with its blue-grey foliage, the blue-to-white spires of *Veronica* 'Blue Charm', and the deep purple leaves of *Heuchera micrantha* 'Palace Purple' with its delicate sprays of dancing white flowers.

Structure is an essential ingredient in any of John's planting schemes. You may come across a vision which appears to be filled with soft textures and colours, but if you look closer you will see that it is always held together by permanent architectural plants within the confines of their borders.

ABOVE: *The sunlight glancing off both the leaves and flower heads of these plants generates a true depth of colour. The daisy heads of* Rudbeckia fulgida, Echinacea purpurea *and* Helianthus atrorubens *all have the same dark eye.*

LEFT: *A view of the sunken hexagonal lily pond shows a more traditional approach to design. Balustraded walls, sweeping steps and an oversized stone ball finial sit atop a brick pillar reminiscent of grand English houses.*

In 1998 the makers of BBC Television's 'Gardeners' World' approached three very different designers with an identical project brief. John Brookes, Bonita Bulaitis (see page 32) and Dan Pearson (see page 108) were each given a virgin oblong plot with few natural benefits in Kings Heath Park, Birmingham and asked to design a garden to be featured in the series. The one common feature between these adjoining gardens was the link to the fields and trees beyond. The designers all acknowledged a responsibility to preserve the environment and to use only materials sympathetic to the plots. All tended to bring the landscape into the garden, thereby extending the small space, rather than inflict the man-made upon it. Another surprise was the selection of trees: without consultation, they all chose silver birches.

Limited budgets made the task more difficult. The results were amazingly dissimilar and personal. Knowing the designers' work, it is easy to recognize their very distinct styles and philosophies, yet even so the gardens demonstrate a fresh approach to garden design by each of them.

Above left: *Coursed brick and blue-stained timber terraces cut into a covering of small rounded shingle and larger pebbles. Permanent planting is supplied by a group of yuccas and the evergreen* Elaeagnus x ebbingei. *White birch trunks provide additional interest in winter.*

Left: *The blue timber decking and fence panel are reflected in the still water of the pool. Bright blue-glazed pots planted with yellow-flowering seasonal plants replicate the colour theme of the garden.*

John's design brings together many of the elements he has used in gardens throughout the world. A strong geometric layout unifies paviors, stained timber decking, gravel, grass and water. His colours are limited to a select few: cool blues reflect the sky and bright yellows bring a quality of light and jollity to the garden. These shades also provide continuity with the fields beyond. By placing grass at the end of the garden, he has naturally stretched the design to take in the field, creating the illusion of length. His love of texture also comes into play, with the longer field grass against the lush cultivated lawn, and the rounded gravel with the larger river-worn cobbles and stones. Squares of dark blue decking linked into angular brick terraces are set round a naturally shaped pool. A pebble beach leads to another decking platform and round a gravelled curve, obscuring

Iris pseudacorus 'Variegata' form great clumps at the pool margins and create a splash of bright colour throughout the summer months.

the view towards the field which has now become part of the garden. This is a smaller version of the rococo gardens of the eighteenth century, but John has replaced the follies with bright patches of colour: a clump of yellow and cream *Iris pseudacorus* 'Variegata' leaves set at the junction of the far blue deck, and the verdant grass with its planting of *Betula jacquemontii*. The still water of the pond makes play with the light.

While John is aware of the need to work with nature, he also knows how to stimulate a passionate response. His designs appear to be simple, but they are truly ingenious. His knowledge and skill are second to none, as his devoted followers will testify.

CHAPTER TWO

Dynamics

The use of geometry contrasting
with naturalistic planting

BONITA BULAITIS

For excitement and intensity in contemporary design we look to Bonita Bulaitis. Her work includes the most unusual and innovative pieces of art, highlighted by the rich vibrancy of colour in her planting. Bonita is an original freethinker. She not only designs gardens, she is happy to pass on her knowledge, both as a lecturer on design development and as a television presenter.

Bonita began as a graphic designer, a field which continues to influence her today. Her use of novel materials and ability to create enchantment from the unusual makes you stand back and re-evaluate what you want from a garden. Bonita's obvious passion for experimenting with the untried pays dividends in full. Her colour sense is that of a true artist. Gertrude Jekyll began life as a watercolourist and was able to use this knowledge to create great drifts of colour with plants. Bonita also abstracts this knowledge and gives us exuberant canvases of texture and vivid colour like no one else's.

Having decided that she wanted to diversify, Bonita began a part-time course on landscape architecture, but she found the way it compartmentalized things immensely frustrating and left to return to her graphic design business. However, it was at this time that computers arrived and changed the face of graphics, and the high cost of computers and software spelt the end of

OPPOSITE: *Back lighting throws the stained glass panels set in the wall into bright relief, while the* Cyperus papyrus, Nandina domestica, *grasses and cascading ivies add a softness to the base.*

ABOVE: *The wonderful colour combination of the flat heads of deep golden yellow* Achillea 'Feuerland' *and wine-purple flowers of* Allium sphaerocephalon *contrast with the pale variegated grass.*

Bonita's graphics business. In the meantime she had caught the gardening bug. Growing all her vegetables in tubs became a passion; they even came with her when she moved house so that she had an instant edible garden.

It was at about this time that she picked up a book on garden design and thought that she could do that. She spent two years working in a garden centre where she was responsible for filling the hanging baskets with eccentric plant combinations. As a result customers began to ask her for garden designs, but she felt unable to do them because she had no formal qualifications. The

outcome was her enrolment at the English Garden School. After qualifying, by her own admission she spent the next four to five years trying to "get back to my soul".

Bonita's effervescent character needs the right environment to allow her inventive and zany ideas to bubble over. She is in her element when she can follow her heart as well as her obsessions. Nothing is more exciting than seeing her extraordinarily progressive show gardens set among those of her peers at an English flower show.

At the 1996 Hampton Court Flower Show we were given our first taste of Bonita's 'soul'. Her garden 'Light on the Edge' is essentially a rectangular site overlaid by an almost circular structure. The planting creates a wild natural effect which is held together by the simplicity of the hard landscaping. The garden is enclosed by curving textured cast walls, some with beautiful hand-made glass panels designed by Bonita's sister Susan. In the sunlight, or when illuminated at night, these explode with jewel-

ABOVE: *In daylight the cool coloured courtyard with* Verbena bonariensis *growing through the dark red leaves of* Phormium tenax Purpureum *is offset by the vivid greens of the grasses.*

like colours. Others craftily conceal the fountain source for 'strings of water' suspended within a window in the walls.

Water can be found in different areas of the garden. Circular pools catch the rain and mirror-lined water channels in the shape of crosses are set into the ground. This surface is also unusual as it is resin-bonded with natural quartzite stone which makes it hard-wearing. All of these elements reflect and refract light. The garden flows naturally between the walls, weaving between the light and airy selection of grasses and deep-coloured perennials.

RIGHT: *In the evening the concealed lighting gives the entire garden a new dimension. The vivid colours of* Knautia macedonica *are reflected in the stained glass while the cantilevered steps throw deep shadows.*

An intuitive designer who is not frightened to make bold strong statements or use bright colours, Bonita is not shy of using that most hated of all materials, concrete. However, hers is no common block walling. Her gardens all utilize unusual materials, but the result is captivating creativity.

Of the three gardens created for the 'Gardeners' World' television series, it was Bonita's that was the most controversial. Both John Brookes's (see page 26) and Dan Pearson's (see page 108) gardens were immediately understandable. Bonita chose to throw bright orange abstract structures into relief against the fields beyond. The garden was more like a piece of living modern art and, as with that idiom, people either loved it or hated it. Many people could not see the reasoning behind it, but for me it was the

most brilliant of the three gardens and deserved more credit. I believe it was the most innovative, stretching the imagination.

Bonita wanted the garden to work visually throughout the seasons as well as at differing times of the day. The richly coloured walls appear to change tone according to the light, casting shadows in the sun and supporting and intensifying the delicate contours of the planting. These walls are important structurally in this small space. They add a dynamic which guides you through the garden, yet they are substantial enough to hide surprises. Circular windows in some of the walls allow tempting glimpses of a special plant or other treats beyond. Like Dan and John, she also used silver birches to unify the garden with the natural planting beyond the site. The species chosen, *Betula*

ermanii, has pinkish-white trunks and orange-brown branches which echo the wall colouring. Another wall has been pierced with numerous holes lined with copper pipes. When they catch the light they gleam wonderfully in the sun, but they really come into their own when they are back-lit and the wall is studded with starry points of light.

The walls lie across the site, allowing for sheltered pockets of planting. A dark grey gravel path intersected by wooden beams and stepping stones gently leads one through the garden. I believe Bonita was the first to use transparent tubes containing bright bubbling water as a water feature. Many of her favourite plants are included in this natural-looking garden, particularly tough species of grasses like the Mexican feather grass *Stipa*

tenuissima, a fine-leafed clump-forming grass which is particularly beautiful with its silky awns and bright green, almost iridescent foliage. Smaller bronze-leafed sedges form satellite clumps around the stipa drifting into the gravel. Other plants have been chosen for their rich colours. *Phormium* 'Bronze Baby' and the low-growing purple-leafed sempervivum mirror the dark reds, while *Achillea* 'Summerwine' and *Kniphofia* 'Shining Sceptre' add zest with their contrasting flower heads.

A small selection of shrubs bring colour and permanency to the scheme. The sacred bamboo *Nandina domestica* is extremely decorative with white flowers and vivid red-tinged leaves in spring and autumn, while the snowy mespilus, *Amelanchier lamarckii*, is a delight throughout the year.

RIGHT: *Raindrops are caught in the soft feathery foliage of the grasses as they arch over to meet the resin-formed tentacles in the stream. A pale blue-green metal spiral appears to float across the water.*

BELOW: *The knitted deep-pink metal spiral laced with blue glass beads delivers a touch of whimsy to the perfectly matched planting of* Achillea millefolium *'Cerise Queen' and* A.m. *'Lilac Beauty'.*

The first thing Bonita does for all her major projects is make a model. This is a unique approach which may be a throwback to her previous career. She visualizes in three dimensions, working on a scaled model of the garden before she commits it to two-dimensional paper. In this way her scale and proportions can be exact, but it allows her a flexibility to modify the plan which she feels she does not achieve with conventional design methods. Her maquettes are works of art in themselves. Modelled in fine detail like a stage or set design, with textures created by papers which Bonita makes herself by hand, they depict the gardens in all their glory prior to installation. Her other strength is her ability to think ahead, to imagine how her design's mood will change when the garden is lit, and what kind of lighting will work to best effect. It is a dramatic and dynamic approach. Bonita's ingenuity is infinite. She is a true trailblazer.

Bonita rents space in a nearly derelict nursery in Hertfordshire. Her studio is a small converted hothouse set in a horticultural nightmare. It is here that she and her partner have transformed several of the polytunnels back into working units where she can grow and nurture many of her beloved plants. Her small glasshouse studio looks out onto drifts of grasses, perennials, clipped box balls and her favourite phormiums. This is also where she finds her inspiration.

In Bonita's 'Voyage of Vitality' show garden at the 1997 Hampton Court Flower Show, the sunray tentacles reach out into a water course which meanders through the garden. This exhibit is full of surprises, with stunning planting complemented by ingenious pieces of art. Knitted wire and beaded spirals made by Jan Truman in shades to match the nearby plants seem to grow out of the ground or skim the water's surface. Cantilevered steps with concealed lighting in their risers lead to a higher terrace with a curving metal and wood bench. A series of static blue and copper fans add verticality behind it. The copper theme is repeated by sinuous threads of copper ribbons laid in the resin. Upright copper pipes cut to varying lengths form undulating metal structures which act as the boundaries.

The garden is a mixture of tantalizing, dynamic textures. Bonita explores their energy and movement through a variety of

methods and materials. As ever, Bonita's planting is held together by pivotal plants like phormiums, yet it appears to have an abandoned looseness which knits it together like an Impressionist painting. Her favourite grasses jostle with achilleas in deep reds and the palest of pink, and the steely blue thistle heads of *Eryngium giganteum* nod alongside *Verbena bonariensis*, while the deep wine-red flowers of *Knautia macedonica* appear like dark stars among the foliage.

A small basement garden in London has benefited from some of her wackier schemes. Once a gloomy dark space, it has been transformed into a bright, light and amusing area. By painting the walls, doors and floors with metallic paints, Bonita has brought the sun down to this level. The light-coloured walls are adorned with sun rays in copper paint. The basement floor and walls are coloured a soft grey, with light-reflective silver powder

mixed into the paint to achieve a feeling of greater space. Silver is also used for the plant containers. Galvanized metal florists' buckets with holes punched in the bottom contain shade-loving plants. Larger planters are fashioned from rope-handled play tubs, while brightly coloured plastic footballs with the tops cut off make cheap, eye-catching planters. The door is painted a deep orange which combines with the plant choices to create a bright splash of colour, bringing life to this out-of-the way corner.

Bonita's is a rare skill. Her gardens are sensual, tactile works of art. There is a great harmony of colour from her plants and materials, as well as a warmth which sometimes seems lacking in our male peers who favour the cooler colour ranges. Her passion and love of unusual textures makes her explore the very bounds of established ideas. I applaud her determination to place garden design in the realms of contemporary art.

CHAPTER THREE

Shapes

Minimalism and classic styling
complemented by sophisticated planting

An architectural background combined with a love of the landscape shines through in Christopher Bradley-Hole's classic yet modern work. Christopher pays meticulous attention to detail; even the smallest imperfection will spoil the whole effect for him. In order to achieve this, it is essential for Christopher to have a close working relationship with his landscape contractor.

Plants and gardens have always fascinated Christopher, but he did not have the opportunity to work with them when he practised as an architect. The catalyst was a post-graduate diploma course he took on the conservation of historic gardens and landscapes run by the Architectural Association and which he found inspirational. He feels that it is only when one is armed with an understanding of the origins of gardens that one can abstract the elements needed for modern design.

Christopher strongly believes that if you are going to change, it is essential to understand the fundamental philosophies behind the time-honoured designs before you can create contemporary gardens. For him modern design is about abstraction and must be built on the foundation of tradition. The proportions he uses in his work are exactly the same as those of classical times, but they are brought up-to-date and then used differently.

While he was still working as an architect, Christopher began to design one or two gardens for his clients. Then in 1993, against fierce competition from the gardening fraternity, he won the opportunity to design the Chelsea garden for the magazine

RIGHT: *An unusual fountain set in a dished cube of pale stone on a bed of chippings is planted with orange marigolds, purple sage and flowering thymes.*

ABOVE: *Great windows have been cut into the walls of this otherwise enclosed garden. Geometric blocks of rich colour in the walls echo the velvet hues of the iris petals.*

Gardens Illustrated to celebrate its first anniversary. Christopher found the entire experience exhilarating, from working with this new magazine and interpreting its needs to the exacting task of building the garden for the show. The resulting garden, 'The Explorers' Roof Garden', was a contemporary decked garden steeped in history that paid tribute to the plant hunters of yesteryear. After these beginnings Christopher moved on and away from the long-established rules laid down by the Royal Horticultural Society. Although his design style has changed a great deal since that time, this original show garden acted as the spur for him. He gradually realized that running an architectural practice was not completely compatible with garden design, and he also found it a struggle to run them in tandem, and so he changed career direction.

The other big influence on him over the past few years has been the planting styles in Europe, especially those in Germany, Holland and Sweden. He has never been interested in shrub and

A raised border in a framework of polished plaster beams alongside a decking path leads across the waterfall and stream.

A simple stone bench surrounded by a planting of irises and cardoons set in gravel reflects the lines of the steel girders.

mixed borders, and the use of perennials allows a new freedom to combine plants in a more modern way, for he has always been fanatical about plants. Christopher Lloyd's garden at Great Dixter was the greatest influence on him as he was able to appreciate that the informal style of planting can still retain a definite structure. In his award-winning 'The Latin Garden' at the 1997 Chelsea Flower Show depicting the life and works of Virgil, Christopher's use of polished plaster and steel combined with gravel beds and mirror-smooth water was incredibly disciplined. It was very far removed from the standard gardens normally seen

at the Show. The whole setting was immensely stimulating with its use of oblongs and squares influencing the three different sections of the layout.

The steel structure and rendered concrete walls would be intimidating if they were not softened by colour-washed polished plaster and the rich velvet colours of the iris used in the planting. Deep browns, blacks and umbers are lightened by touches of

The mirror-still oblong pool creates the division between the garden and the mild steel structure framing the covered terrace.

white and yellow, pale mauve-blues and the silver-grey foliage plants. A steeply stepped waterfall allows the play of light to add the only movement and brilliancy to the stillness of the garden.

Christopher's planting selection is pure Mediterranean in feel, enhanced by twisted olive trees and vines. Structured shapes in the leaf forms of the irises and *Cynara cardunculus*, in combination with the regimented planting of the *Cupressus sempervirens* and poplar trees, are all evocative of Italy. These are softened by the relaxed style of the herbaceous planting set randomly in gravel beds. The soft colour tones are enhanced by the exotic flower heads of angelica and cardoons. The use of geometry in the planting echoes the strict majesty of the strong verticals of the girders. The grey of the iris leaves reflects the colour tones of the mild steel.

This is real drama translated into a garden. Classic shapes are complemented by the use of modern materials. The combinations of verticals and horizontals, squares and rectangles, and their interactions and reflections with light, combine to make the mood within the garden change subtly. Christopher's attention to detail, his innovative use of materials not normally associated with intimate gardens, and his exact use of colour unify the whole.

This is not an unfriendly garden. Often we are put off by the use of concrete and metal within the garden framework. We tend to associate them with ugly industrial developments or perhaps feel that they are too clinical for us to be at ease with them. These are our own prejudices and they frequently blind us.

Christopher's work is very far removed from these concepts. He creates beautiful living spaces from these materials that we resist so strongly. The architectural shapes are timeless. His use of simple uncluttered forms proves that we really do not need to add a multitude of curves and frills to create a garden.

If we open our eyes and see stunning British designs such as 'The Latin Garden' clearly, landscape and garden design will start moving into a new era. The use of such materials has been translated successfully in the garden environment in America and Australasia, but it is an uphill struggle to use them in the smaller garden plots of Europe. Nevertheless, Christopher continues to experiment with using modern materials and with implementing these minimalist schemes.

clipped box balls

perennial
planting

multi-stemmed
birch tree

magnolia tree in
neighbouring
garden

upper terrace

conservatory

house

The ground plan shows the elegant simplicity of this minimalist garden in Chelsea with its structured brick walls, terracing and topiary.

Architecture and the related disciplines are currently undergoing a second wave of modernism which picks up on traditions in a new way. Designers such as Tadao Ando, Daniel Liebeskind and Piet Oudolf affect the way in which we perceive our work. As an architect, Christopher became bogged down with commercial projects and fell out of love with architecture, but he found that once he left this environment for the garden, his passion for good modern architecture was rekindled and recently he has been able to bring this into play in his work. Confidence comes with knowing your subject, so it is the designer's role to lead clients and reassure them about design, though often full comprehension can only come about when a garden is complete. Clients, too, are taking a risk in trying out new things and need to be encouraged. Christopher has the self-assurance to inspire his forward-thinking clients. His background enables him to tie in the garden design plans with the existing house and so he can suggest altering a structure with confidence.

Christopher's clients come to him because they are attracted to his contemporary style. Many of them live in traditional English houses, but want to do so in a more modern way. He passionately believes that his style sits equally well with both new and old established buildings. His wish is to design good lasting gardens in a modern way.

He agrees that there is something undeniably attractive in a traditional garden, but argues that there is also a need to move forward. Interiors are becoming less fussy and more clean-cut, and gardens must also respond to this movement. One of Christopher's current projects is designing a garden for a client in the Cotswolds. This is a beautiful part of England, steeped in heritage and tradition, and much loved by tourists. His theme is simple: cut back to the bare minimum and use natural materials wherever possible. He has used decking and a mixture of sawn and cut Cotswold stone, combined with a little reconstituted stone, to make the base for a garden that will be very structured. The garden is in proportion with its environment and has a natural hierarchy about it.

A small London garden in Chelsea is one of his most recent commissions. The garden is quite minimalist, mirroring the interior. Christopher describes it as "a bit like taking the

LEFT: *The architectural lines of the retaining walls emulate the foundations. Their simplicity and colour picks up that of the wall, providing the garden with both structure and continuity.*

RIGHT: *The massed planting of evergreen clipped box balls forms a focal point from the house. Terracotta pots also planted with box continue the structural and colour theme.*

LEFT: *Plain terracotta 'punch bowls' have been filled with the evergreen succulent* sempervivum *and a permanent planting of herbs.*

RIGHT: *The simplicity of the rows of box balls is arresting. They catch the sunlight which causes their shape to be thrown into relief against the wall.*

foundations out into the garden". There are a number of knee-high brick walls enclosing beds, and a simple space in the middle looking back towards the house. It has been planted up quite loosely with his beloved perennials and grasses, except for a collection of regimented clipped box balls which are used as the focal point of the garden.

The back wall and a wall in the conservatory have been rendered with polished plaster in a warm earthy red tone that echoes the colour of the brick. This technique, which uses ground marble containing crystals which both reflect and absorb the colour, is currently being used by only one man in England. Eventually a series of inscribed stone plaques by Belinda Eade will be set onto the garden wall.

Christopher enjoys working and sharing ideas with artists from other disciplines. He and Belinda have collaborated on a number of projects, including his first Chelsea garden. He always tries to place a piece of art within a scheme, as he did with the

stone plaques inscribed with the works of Virgil which were scattered liberally around 'The Latin Garden'.

Christopher admits it takes courage and trust on the part of a client to commission a piece of modern art for the garden. A designer may be able to explain what is required, but he will relinquish control when he hands the project over. Ultimately it is the artist who will interpret the brief and deliver the piece. There is an element of risk here as this is an unknown quantity, but this is what makes it so special. It is up to the designer to persuade a client to abandon the well-worn path of placing a traditional piece within a garden. When a really fine new piece of art is unveiled a tremendous sense of joy is released.

Christopher brings a refreshing approach to garden design. Gone are the traditional mores. He has made us look deeper into our psyche and realize that we need to revise our way of thinking, even to the point where plans are honed to such a degree that they are almost gardenless. His is a new age of minimalism.

ABOVE: *A black-stained pergola supports a scented rose bower, the rich pinks complemented by perennial underplanting of Polygonum affine 'Donald Lowndes', purple sage, alchemilla and purple foxgloves. Balance is achieved by introducing* Cotinus coggygria *and philadelphus.*

LEFT: *A single-flowered rose tumbles over the raised wall of the pool garden, while the fragrant arbour provides a shaded seating area.*

CHAPTER FOUR

Soul

Wild flowers and nature combined to evoke
a sense of peace and tranquility

JULIE TOLL

Julie Toll has a special place in the hearts of all visitors to the Chelsea Flower Show. Her show gardens are a delight: always different, sometimes shocking, occasionally controversial. First trained as a horticulturist, she took a course at the English School of Garden Design, set up her garden design practice and has never looked back. Her speciality appears unique: Julie combines a very natural style with an unsurpassed knowledge of wild flowers. Even the most formal and English of her gardens will include a grass meadow, bringing the design back from whence it came, namely nature.

The warmth of Julie's planting schemes is reminiscent of an earlier age, but her plant selection is not. Here she uses a cleverly restricted palette of colour to achieve an arbour of all shades of pink. Roses clamber over a black-stained pergola, deepest pink to the palest of pale. A symphony of colour is picked up by the deep purple hues of *Cotinus coggygria* 'Royal Purple' and pink and white foxglove flowers. The vibrant lime green of *Alchemilla mollis* and white fragrant flowers of *Philadelphus* 'Virginal' add splashes of light, while the dark purple of a large-flowered clematis adds depth. The roses and arbour extend into the swimming pool garden, while the alchemilla reappears in the white garden. The pink of the roses is repeated in the standard roses in the parterre.

ABOVE AND RIGHT: *The formality of the mown lawn and clipped parterre contrasts with meadow grass, while informal planting in the white garden provides a cool and tranquil setting.*

Originally designed for the Chelsea Flower Show, 'The Eros Garden' has a permanent site within the Royal Horticultural Society's Garden at Wisley in Surrey. A very geometric garden planned round a series of circles, each section interlocks, but each has a different bias. Formal landscaping with stone edging delineates paths, paving and borders. Softened by a fusion of native planting and modern shrubs, it draws the eye to a cupola and circular pond. Again it is the magic of Julie's planting which brings joy to this small garden. The combination of many of our common wild flowers with cultivated plants creates a tapestry in the flowering lawn. The lawn is situated in front of a border of striking shrubs so the delicate flowers are offset by the large leaves in the background.

Natural stone paths sweep round colour-themed borders and meet curved paths constructed from rounded pebbles which enclose smaller, more intricate planting. The entire garden is linked by the water feature. The pool with its statue of Eros feeds a shallow water channel that moves diagonally across the garden to encircle the cupola. The channel is lined with river-washed

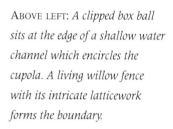

ABOVE LEFT: *A clipped box ball sits at the edge of a shallow water channel which encircles the cupola. A living willow fence with its intricate latticework forms the boundary.*

LEFT: *Strap-leafed variegated* sisyrinchium, *and* Iris pallida *'Variegata' with is pale mauve-blue scented flowers, are grouped together with low-growing thymes, their shapes reflected by the delicate grass* Festuca glauca.

ABOVE & RIGHT: *The original planting includes white-flowered wisteria over the cupola,* Pittosporum tenuifolium, *white nicotiana,* Veronica gentianoides, *grasses and artemisia to create a very cool scheme.*

pebbles, a smaller version of the stones used in the paths, their natural colours intensified by the water.

The planting has changed and adjusted to its permanent home, but the original mood has not been lost. The garden has thousands of visitors, so the plants must be tough enough to survive. Evergreen planting around the boundary provides framework and structure for the less hardy plants. *Prunus laurocerasus,* our common laurel with big leathery leaves, combines with the small pale green leaves of *Pittosporum tenuifolium* from New Zealand to make an impenetrable screen, while in another corner a grouping of bamboos and ferns allows the wind to rustle their leaves. Other shrubs are sited to punctuate the planting. Two *Hebe buxifolia,* rounded evergreen shrubs with rich shiny leaves and white flowers, sit sentinel on either side of a bench.

Julie and John Chambers, who is famous for his wild flower seeds, combined to make a successful partnership over the years which brought Julie to the forefront of British garden design. She was the first designer to use wild flower mixtures successfully at the Chelsea Flower Show, and for a while this became her trademark. The vibrant colours of bright red poppies against white feverfew flowers and blue cornflowers evoked such memories of our cornfields that everyone wanted to copy this formula.

Using wild flowers in a garden takes time and patience. An awareness of both the natural habitat of flowers and the ground conditions is essential, and Julie's knowledge of the plants and love of nature shines through. Their garden designed to attract butterflies expanded on this theme. Poppies were still evident but a patch of daisy-strewn grass was added, along with massed plantings of *Viola tricolor* and *Veronica gentianoides*, bright blue speedwell. A more muted woodland feel was achieved the following year with lovely combinations of massed cowslips and water avens, interspersed with the beautiful bright yellow and green striped leaves of *Iris pseudacorus* 'Variegata'. With its dense planting, tree canopy and water, this garden was a haven for birds.

ABOVE: *Blue cornflowers, red poppies and white feverfew stir the emotions in the 1990 Chelsea Flower Show garden.*

LEFT: *Butterfly-attracting plants mix with the white and pink campions, bedstraw, spikes of blue speedwell and tall yellow mullein in the 1991 Chelsea Flower Show garden.*

RIGHT: *The muted colours of the woodland and pond-side planting provide a haven for small animals and birds in the 1992 Chelsea Flower Show garden.*

Water plays an essential role in any garden and is especially evocative among wild flower planting. Julie's garden at the Hampton Court Flower Show demonstrates how a small space can be turned into a truly inspirational one. Dry-stone walling forms the rear of the pool. Water feeds the pond through an old pump which splashes into a large copper bowl and on into the muddy pool. There is a marginal planting of willows, common cotoneaster, and ferns with the added exuberance of wild flower colours. Pale pink *Polygonum bistorta*, pink stickleweed, mountain arnica with its bright yellow flowerheads, the blue of meadow cranesbill and creeping campanulas all combine harmoniously. And still there is space enough for a simple clay brick terrace and a hammock in which to relax.

In contrast, the large sweep of simple daisy-strewn meadow grass bounding a farm lake is superbly restful. Fewer flower species have been used and greater emphasis has been placed on the grasses. On the far side of the lake a water meadow and masses of candelabra primulas, *Primula pulverulenta* and *P. sikkimensis*, have been used to create the feel of wild flower planting. Both wild and cultivated flowers have been cleverly mixed in this meadow to achieve just the right atmosphere. This is the English countryside in all its glory, a fake none the less, but one created by an artist.

LEFT: *Swathes of grass are mown through the flower meadow to create paths down to the lake. The smooth grass provides a textural contrast to the rougher meadow.*

LEFT: *Ox-eye daisies and long meadow grass lead down to the lake. Looking across to the farm buildings, giant euphorbias are in flower, reflecting the bright sunlight.*

ABOVE: *The breeze causes the long grass to wave and rustle. Each flower head catches the sunlight, looking as though it is dancing around the massed planting of primulas in the water meadow.*

A giant sculpture of reclaimed timber designed to resemble a giant seed pod hangs in the depth of the woodland. This arresting contemporary sculpture blends perfectly with the natural surroundings.

A beaten path through the forest is flanked by massed drifts of shade-loving plants: lacy woodruff, lady's mantle, light blue-flowered corydalis, dark blue bugle and the bright orange of kingcups.

Challenging natural sculptures frequently find their way into Julie's gardens, pushing at the boundaries of our imagination. Organic shapes and structures, like the giant seed pods which hang from tree trunks in her 'Forest Garden', are chosen for their ability to blend with her naturalistic style as well as to show off modern sculpture at its most intriguing. Julie's sensitivity to the environment is apparent in all her designs, but especially so in this garden where she has managed to capture the very essence of a forest and its microclimate. Anyone wanting to create a woodland garden can take stock of what flourishes under these conditions, and which plants mix together to form a colourful blanket of flowers.

There are many misconceptions about shady gardens, the main one being that very little will grow, and only boring plants at that. This garden turns this assumption on its head. The colour is really for one season, late spring through early summer when dappled light can still penetrate the leaf canopy and warm the

Beaten tracks lead up to the log cabin and an old Swedish chair. White foxgloves and downy stems of verbascum provide touches of light.

soil, but what a delight it is. The moisture-loving *Corydalis flexuosa* 'Pere David', its true blue flowers and lacy leaves mixed with the bright lime green of *Alchemilla mollis*, the delicate white flowers of woodruff, *Galium odoratum*, and startling, bright yellow-orange flowers of *Geum elatum* 'Georgenburg', combine with the dark blue flower spikes of *Ajuga reptans* 'Catlin's Giant' to create an eye-stopping picture. Once the season for flowers has finished, one is left with leaf forms, textures and seed heads that have a beauty and charm all their own.

Gardens like these are also havens for wildlife, generating thickets for small animals and birds, and food for foraging. Natural leaf mould leaves a protective layer to the forest floor and also acts as a source of soil nutrients for future years. Lessons can be learnt here. After all, what is a garden?

LEFT: Pennisetum *'Burgundy Blaze'*, the dark-coloured fountain grass and bright daisy-flowered mesembryanthemum grow freely in the natural crevices formed by rough-hewn local rocks.

BELOW: *A cobble and brick driveway curves past steps to a pergola and tennis court. Intense purple bougainvillea and blue plumbago scramble over the banks while royal palms form stately columns along the drive.*

ABOVE: *The bright blue of the sea is reflected by the swimming pool where giant green-glazed pots decorate the terrace. Tall flower spikes of aloes lend exotic interest to the border.*

RIGHT: *A large copper bowl sits on the driveway, its colour picked up by the massed planting of* Heliconia psittacorum *and flame-coloured flowers of* Delonix regia.

BELOW RIGHT: *An interesting feature has been made of a path leading to a flight of weathered stone steps. Diagonally laid setts have grass joints which help soften the edge of the new stones.*

Under the tropical sun, looking out over the sea with its deep blue light-reflecting waters, waves lapping the beach, there is a very different Julie Toll garden, but one which still follows her philosophy of environmental awareness. Great care has been taken to source and use local materials and place planting schemes to fit the nature of the island. Instead of birch trees there are royal palms, *Roystonea regia*, with their extraordinary swollen bases and green crownshafts. Tough wind-resistant shrubs planted in drifts in the lawn provide protection for the more tender plants. Large rough-hewn rocks give cover for graceful clumps of bronze-leafed grasses, *Pennisetum* 'Burgundy Blaze' aptly named 'fountain grass', which dance in the breeze and glisten in the sunlight.

There are large expanses of cooling green lawn here to soothe the senses. Clumps of aloes with tall orange spikes and bright purple bougainvillea grow exceptionally well under these conditions. To counterbalance the hot tropical colours and the heat, there is an unexpected cool corner where a large clump of carex nestles round the base of a palm. Grass is encouraged to grow through the joints of a sett path towards a short flight of natural weather-worn stone steps leading to a lawn terrace.

LEFT & BELOW: *Sedges growing through sand, creeping yellow buttercups and pink-flowered soapwort with spiky outcrops of sea buckthorn and thrift peeking out of rocky crevices are evocative of childhood.*

Was it a garden or wasn't it? It still won Best Garden in Show at Chelsea in 1993, but the jury and public were divided. 'The Wildflower and Seaside Garden' wasn't so much a garden as a collection of flora in a typical seaside habitat, all beautifully integrated with a bit of lateral thinking. Worn grass tracks weave through the dunes, grading into a sandy path leading down to the beach, past rabbit burrows planted with nettles, ragwort, plantains, cranesbill and scarlet pimpernel. Scrambling over and through the rocks are hardy thrift, campions, bladderwort and rest-harrow. These plants are not just wild flowers; all of them can be used in modern schemes, especially in coastal areas.

Over the years, Julie has proved to be a thought-provoking designer. In all of her work she uses her extensive knowledge of wild flowers and ecology to create the most beautiful and innovative gardens, and yet each one is distinctive.

LEFT: *Wild strawberries, pink herb robert, white and pink campions and dark blue columbine form a carpet of wild flowers.*

CHAPTER FIVE

Energy

Iconoclastic design where shape, texture
and form take on a new dimension

CLEVE WEST AND JOHNNY WOODFORD

ABOVE: Johnny's carved wooden seat with its oversized ball feet and armrests first saw light in 'The Green Man Garden' at Hampton Court. Now in Cleve's garden, it provides a perfect place for relaxation.

I s this the cutting edge of garden design? A garden or a setting for installation art? Perhaps this is a combination of the two. In any case, it is certainly very different, filled with masculine energy, mind-shatteringly bright primary colours, verdant plants and a rich plethora of unusual, almost primitive artefacts. These are the trademarks of one of Britain's most successful partnerships: Cleve West, garden designer and Johnny Woodford, sculptor. Since their original collaboration at the 1994 Hampton Court Flower Show, they have turned the gardening world upside down. Their views, ideals and sense of humour so match each other that it is strange to realize that Cleve and Johnny have not been working in partnership for very long.

Having been an outstanding athlete as a schoolboy, Cleve seemed destined for a career in sport until he was injured. Nevertheless, he also had a strong leaning towards painting, printing and sculpture. It was therefore natural for him to decide to read for a degree in both physical education and art, though he found that the physical side took up so much time that art was squeezed into the background.

After Cleve left university he could not find a teaching job, but he soon found a position with the fine art publisher Petersberg Press which handled many contemporary artists such as David

LEFT: A wild meadow-style planting grows on the shed roof in Cleve's garden, creating a novel garden arch. Great wooden pods open to form seats in front of the pool with its water-jointed setts and stepping stones.

Hockney and Robert Motherwell. Cleve maintains that he learned more in this year of odd-jobbing in the fine art business than he did in the three he spent at university. His sense of scale and perspective were enhanced as he cut mounts and arranged exhibits for the featured artists, and he also had the good fortune to work in Hockney's studio 'just clearing up'.

Then one day the owner of Petersberg Press asked him to look after his wisteria, and that was the beginning of Cleve's gardening career. At the same time an elderly aunt in Chiswick asked him to help with the upkeep of her garden, so whenever he had time to spare he went in to do some weeding and sorting out. Up to this point Cleve had had no interest in gardening at all, but he found that it became addictive. For a while the pull of sport lured him back into a sports management course, but he continued to work in his aunt's garden. After a couple of years he was hooked and gave up sports management for garden maintenance. At this point he was really just bluffing, as he was only beginning to distinguish a weed from a cultivated plant. A landscaper friend

In Johnny's garden iron wall baskets filled with green Ophiopogon planiscapus *hang from the brightly painted wall. Below it a zebra-striped fish sculpture doubles as a seat beneath a small bed planted with delicate* Polystichum setiferum *ferns.*

then taught him how to lay paving and build walls, and from there it was a natural progression into hard landscaping and then, finally, the transition into 'design and build'.

In the late eighties Cleve went to the Chelsea Flower Show, but he found that the gardens on show held very little interest for him. Nonetheless, the experience stirred the latent artist in him and he decided to go on a design course. He chose the course run by John Brookes at the garden design school at Kew partly because it was near to his home, but also because he admired John's work and thought it would be beneficial to be tutored by such an experienced, eminent modern thinker.

John proved to be an excellent teacher. His clarity of thought and teaching methods made Cleve realize that he had already been taught these principles in a less insightful way at college and that he had been wasting his time by not implementing them before. He found John's methods magical. John stimulated discussion among his students which encouraged them to look into the future rather than over their shoulders into the past.

It was indirectly through John that he met the sculptor Johnny Woodford, as a friend of John's collected artworks which included Johnny's furniture. At this time Cleve was considering his first Hampton Court show garden, 'The Green Man Garden', and he was searching for a source of wood from a sustainable forest to make environmentally friendly furniture. She gave him Johnny's details and the rest, as they say, is history.

Many of the spoils left over from the shows find permanent homes back in the gardens of the designers concerned. Cleve's own garden is no exception. His design, a simple one to suit a modern townhouse, was adapted to utilize many of the features he had used in 'The Green Man Garden'. The garden is divided into two distinct sections by a dramatic water feature which stretches across its width. This rectangular pool is fed by water dripping from a series of Johnny's carved wooden planters set at the ends of the pool. Stepping stones lead through the water, under an archway created by the overhang of the shed roof, into a secluded, sunken paved area at the rear of the garden.

Painted and plain augers, carved wooden balls, phormiums and ferns all appear to grow out of a mulch of rusting iron chains at the base of the bright orange wall in Johnny's garden.

Architectural plants dominate this small space, but there is still room for a wild flower meadow – on top of the reinforced shed roof. There are so many quirky features in this tiny space that it is hard to know where to begin.

A mix of reclaimed landscaping materials, York stone slabs, granite setts and washed pea shingle all blend to make up the backbone. Unusually, the stained black shed sits centrally in the garden, forming a natural dividing line between the pool and the sunken area to the rear. Johnny's wonderful pods unfold to make bizarre seats next to the house, while his reclaimed elm bench is set among exotic leaf forms to provide a relaxing spot at the end of the garden. No prissy planting here: *Acanthus hungaricus*, *Phormium tenax* and *Yucca recurvifolia* all make wonderful statements with their architectural leaves. Cool greens and natural earth tones of wood and stone create a powerful and yet tranquil setting for a busy designer.

Johnny's garden, however, is far from quiet; it is possibly one of the most riotous gardens ever created. It reflects his work as an artist and is filled with his sculptures. Basically this is another dour, dark, tiny basement with all the problems that go with it, but they have conceived this as an area in which to display Johnny's talents to the full. Many brightly painted, larger than life wooden forms in amazing shapes, a fish bench, chunky wooden 'cannon balls', and a door with an oversized keyhole worthy of Alice's Wonderland all combine to make this a spirited garden. It has such as sense of the ridiculous that you cannot help grinning with delight.

A small selection of plants that survive this inhospitable space are helped by the addition of a mulch covering. But since this is Johnny's garden, this is no ordinary mulch but more an artwork of carefully arranged iron chains. As the sun has difficulty reaching this intimate space, one wall has been painted the most vibrant orange, while another one at a lower level has been covered in sheets of galvanized steel to transform an ugly but essential load-bearing wall. Like Cleve's own garden, Johnny's reflects the great sense of humour and style of its owner.

A raised planting bed made out of logs and carved elm salvaged from diseased wood spills over with a mix of blue fescues, crocosmia and herbs to create an unusual feature within 'The Green Man Garden'.

The storms of 1987 and 1990, combined with the effects of Dutch elm disease, ravaged the English countryside. Beautiful ancient trees were lost at a single blow. Much of the wood was wasted, but a new life was waiting for some of it. Many artists, sculptors, furniture makers and joiners found it a great source of material. Some rare species of trees which normally would be unobtainable became available. So the devastation had a few compensations.

Johnny Woodford has a very individual approach to sculpture. Many of his objects are naïve in style, evocative of childhood when everything seems to take on a larger than life dimension. Some are reminiscent of primitive tribal pieces, and all are bold and tactile. He does not restrict his work to one particular area, but moves happily from creating a huge abstract piece with no real function, to furniture that can double as a piece of art or be used as a chair or table. All of it is taken from the remnants of those demolished trees.

Cleve first met Johnny when he was putting together the elements for 'The Green Man Garden' for the 1994 Hampton Court Flower Show. This was April: the show was in July. Cleve still lacked the environmentally friendly furniture he required and feared that no one could make the pieces he needed in time. He had admired Johnny Woodford's work in a client's garden, and when they met they quickly discovered that they held similar views on art and design. Most importantly, they found that they shared a sense of humour. I understand this well myself. It is all too easy to lose our sense of perspective and get things out of proportion, and to take ourselves too seriously. Cleve and Johnny work well as a team because they have such a similar outlook.

Johnny rose to the occasion and made the seats and other items for 'The Green Man Garden', and the two went on to win the George Cooke Award for the most original and innovative show garden. It took the visitors, judges and other designers into a totally new world where the garden is a platform for installation art. The plants, hard landscaping and specially commissioned artefacts all work holistically. Each item is important, but each needs the infrastructure to place it in the right context.

The Thames Water Company sponsored their next two show gardens, 'The Water Wise Gardens'. This gave them the exceptional opportunity to have a show place to consolidate their talents and to give us two incredibly different, bizarre gardens. It was immediately obvious that their confidence in their partnership had grown during the previous three years.

The first of these gardens is a zany mixture of tropical planting style and daffy wooden pieces, with rusting metal and plastic structures straight out of a child's imagination. An immense wooden arm topped with a spiky ball acts as a water fountain feeding water into a pool constructed from giant plastic pipes. Further plastic pipes snake around the whole garden, linked by undulating oversized fence boards, past abstract pieces of Johnny's work 'flying off' into the distance. Huge metal tubes set at drunken angles have yuccas sprouting out of their tops, while chunky wooden kites appear to be anchored to the ground by a ball and chain. The whole garden is so surreal that you can really lose yourself in it. Imagination allowed to run riot. Needless to say, this garden again walked off with a host of awards, including 'the most innovative of the show'.

An enormous black arm looms over the first 'Water Wise Garden'. This is the feed to the purple-spiked fountain which spills water into a pool made from coils of black plastic piping which are set in gravel.

By their third show garden we were all expecting to be shocked, stimulated and excited by the West-Woodford exhibit. And we were not disappointed. Once again the theme is based on water conservation, and their clever understated use of running water is inspirational. The pagan feel of their gardens firmly places them apart from the more contemporary exhibits that seem to come from an entirely different school of thought, espousing a clinical minimalism almost bereft of colour and plants. In contrast, the West-Woodford gardens are exuberant.

There is an inherently tribal quality in their schemes, and this one conjures up the feeling of an African kraal protected by spear-carriers. Although there are no spears, we are greeted by a framework of fierce stakes curving outwards to repel invaders. A sturdy sculptural fence protects the inner sanctum. And what a sanctuary. Curving paths and steps lead down to a heart that exudes such peace that you could hardly believe that you were in the middle of the busiest flower show in Europe.

Water is used cunningly, flowing from a rather unusual gargoyle over setts and gravel into a completely still pool. The pool lies in the centre of clusters of grasses, including the very

LEFT AND ABOVE: *Grey gravel mounds supporting thin cypress trees and fluid sculptures sit in the drought-loving garden, while massed planting of alliums, herbs and yuccas provide a lush contrast in the raised beds at the centre of the garden.*

pretty red-leafed Japanese blood grass *Imperata cylindrica* 'Red Baron' and grey-leafed yuccas. Dry-laid grey granite setts form gently contoured raised beds which curve round to embrace the plants and hide the pool from immediate discovery. Grey granite chippings form the paths and act as a mulch, integrating the different portions of the garden.

Unlike Cleve and Johnny's previous gardens, this one has no bright paint, only the natural colours of the different woods enhanced by the colours of the plants and gravel mulches, so that the plants and sculptures are seen in a more naturalistic way. They do not compete, but complement each other. Only natural materials have been used. Wood, stone, metals and plants are in complete harmony. This also enables you to imagine how you could use these elements in your own garden. Here many of Johnny's pieces of sculpture seem to burst out of spherical wooden pods. These are stunning in isolation, but taken as a collection they seem to be a jokey version of plants exploding out of the soil. Other pieces are rather more frightening, like the spears and the rather strange 'wasp sting' that appears to grow out of a black wooden vase.

It is in this garden that we are really able to appreciate Cleve's inventive planting schemes, like the single, tall slender Mediterranean cypress growing out of a volcano of chippings. Other areas are packed with an eclectic selection of plants: small blue grey-leafed yuccas, rosemary and thyme, the silver flower heads of Miss Wilmott's ghost, *Eryngium giganteum*, and the huge rounded seed heads of *Allium albopilosum* illuminated by the bright gold of *Carex elata* 'Aurea', a golden sedge.

This garden has a depth of feeling that made many people sit up and rethink their views on contemporary garden design. It still takes a brave non-commercial client to install a garden on these lines. Happily, Johnny and Cleve are currently working on an outdoor installation with Sue Sutherland for the Artsway Project near Lymington in the New Forest in Hampshire, a lottery-funded arts centre that is now nearing completion

Both also continue to practise their arts independently. Cleve designs contemporary gardens where he likes to liven them up by including a piece of modern art, preferably one of Johnny's. Meanwhile, Johnny creates his unique pieces of sculpture for those people who really appreciate his style. Thanks to the attention generated by their show gardens, nowadays they are able to attract clients who are particularly interested in gardens where both can utilize their craft.

Their work is unconventional, but it is also stimulating. It may not appeal to everyone, but it makes you reconsider exactly what a garden is. And what you want from one. It is regrettable that not many clients are adventurous enough to install one of Cleve and Johnny's gardens, but it is already clear that they are very much part of the modern movement.

A great explosion of arrows bursts out of the central sculpture in the calm interior of the garden, while a bizarre wooden gargoyle pours water onto setts and gravel that feed the pool.

CHAPTER SIX

Spirit

Architectural discipline
at one with the environment

DEBBIE ROBERTS & IAN SMITH OF ACRES WILD

When two people are on the same wavelength, the result can be a really impressive partnership. This was certainly true for Debbie Roberts and Ian Smith who met while each was reading for a degree in landscape architecture. They soon realized that no one else in their year had the same concern for ecology or wanted to work in a more naturalistic way, and so they teamed up for a course project. They continued to work together throughout their university days and subsequently set up Acres Wild, their successful landscape design partnership, in Sussex.

Debbie and Ian consider the interaction of people within the environment to be an essential ingredient for an optimum design. Armed with a thorough knowledge of the lie of the land, these two have created some of the most successful contemporary

ABOVE: *Tiny cobbles set in concrete surround a bed filled with the dark purple leaves of a bugle and the contrasting bright green of the architectural hosta leaves.*

LEFT: *A square reflecting pool fed by a slate rill is central to the space. The source is a drilled stone bowl set in cobbles brimming over with water.*

RIGHT: *The trees are reflected in the mirrored surface of the pool, while the water flowing down the rill steps does not even make a ripple to disturb the tranquility.*

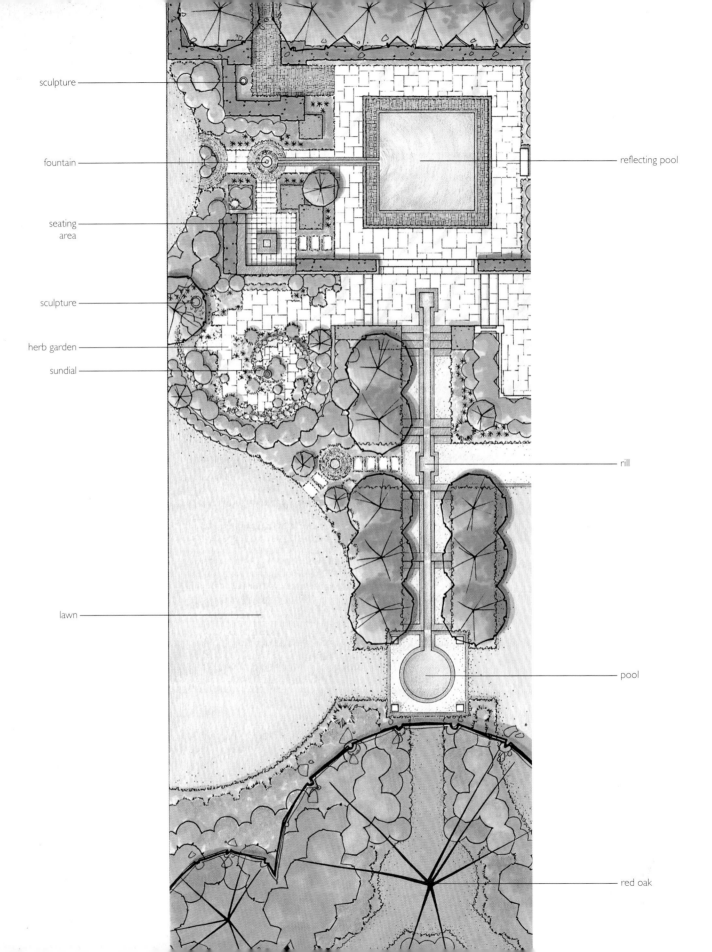

sculpture

fountain

seating
area

sculpture

herb garden

sundial

lawn

reflecting pool

rill

pool

red oak

ABOVE AND RIGHT: *Based on feng shui, the principal rill is oriented on a north-south axis centred on an existing giant red oak.* BELOW RIGHT: *The outdoor seating area has fine views of the surrounding countryside.*

country gardens in England. Both feel passionately that their skills are more in sympathy with the countryside.

The clean strong lines of architecture are influential in all their work. Bold, simple geometry is the trigger for the development of their garden plans into which they introduce creative spaces where specific activities take place. They develop a close working relationship with their clients and, from the site analysis and a detailed client brief, they are able to consider the garden's design and construction holistically.

The house of their clients in Surrey had been built around the principles of feng shui and the garden had to encompass them as well. The house, a new Georgian-style property, has extensive views to the south. Debbie and Ian divided the garden into two distinct halves. The formal garden, 'to heal the body and uplift the spirit', is actually an arrangement of interlinked spaces with a series of water gardens bounding the house. These elements are surrounded by a sweeping formal lawn and deep borders which act as the boundary between the formality of the terraces and the informality of the meadows and rock garden. The latter leads down to the free-form pool which lies in a natural gradient at the bottom of the garden.

A great red oak dominates the garden and provides the focal point for an elegant stepped rill that progresses down to a

perfectly circular pool which is centred directly on the tree. The rill has been set on a north-south axis. Edged with sawn silver-green slate coping stones, it is precise in its direction in order to conform to the principles of feng shui. The same slate is used in the meditation garden, bringing a continuity of colour and materials to the formal water gardens. The rill itself is a series of steps and terraces with square pools containing simple fountains which create concentric circles of water. By way of contrast, the circular pool is a mirror of still dark water which catches the reflection of the oak.

The meditation garden on the very highest terrace is equally symmetrical; it is carefully aligned at right angles with the stepped rill. A brimming circular stone bowl set in a surround of marble cobbles feeds a narrow rill that in turn drops into a square reflecting pool set in front of the house. A plain stone bench has been placed as the focus of the rill. The geometric lines of the

paving form a contemporary parterre with minimalist planting of clipped box to emphasize the simplicity of the overall design. Bright blue bugle, large clumps of iris, shuttlecock heads of ferns and giant hosta leaves all act as a calming influence in front of the ornate flowering rhododendrons. Great blocks of evergreen laurel hedging have been planted as screens and windbreaks for a sheltered seating area which overlooks a herb garden.

The herb garden is less austere and has been designed around a spiral theme. Herbs jostle one another through beds covered by cobbles within the contrasting fomality of rectangular Indian sandstone slabs. The informality is heightened by the introduction of a sculpture of 'Daisy' who sits beneath a weeping silver-leafed pear pouring water from a conch shell onto the pebbles below.

The borders in the lower garden are filled with soft colours from massed lavenders, rosemaries, white flowering potentillas and cotton lavender.

LEFT: *A specially commissioned sundial with a tortoise carrying the world on his back occupies a central position within the herb garden.*

RIGHT: *Giant rhododendrons and the beautiful silver-leafed weeping pear form the perfect backdrop to the intimate planting of herbs.*

More often than not modern developers do not take the environment into consideration when they build a new estate, industrial or domestic, or even a single residence. Frequently they jam as many houses as is physically possible into a spare acre of land. The garden does not seem to be as important to the quality of life as the actual house. Of course this is financially led; there is no altruism here.

An empathetic architect may locate the structure so that its main windows and doors look out towards the view, but this will not necessarily be the right orientation for the garden, and frequently there is no discernible link to the surrounding countryside. It is rare for an architect or developer to consult with a landscape architect or garden designer before work starts. It is when there is a two way discussion, or even a three way one when a client has commissioned the house, about the orientation, house, garden and the world beyond the boundary that the spirit of the site is released.

Both Debbie and Ian feel passionately that there must be congruence between all these factors. The house must fit the garden and the garden must sit happily within the landscape to create a total picture. When they were commissioned to design and implement the garden for a continental-style residence with views of the glorious Sussex Downs, they instinctively knew that their approach had to be bold. A dramatic contemporary garden was essential if it was to interact with the natural scenery and not be lost against the strong, dominant structure of the house.

The architect-designed house was constructed from dark red bricks and dark blue engineering bricks in a very contemporary

LEFT: *Water grasses blend with the border plantings to soften the rigid lines of the pool.*

RIGHT: *A fountain of grass seed heads spills over a rock at the corner of a flight of steps leading to the semicircular pool.*

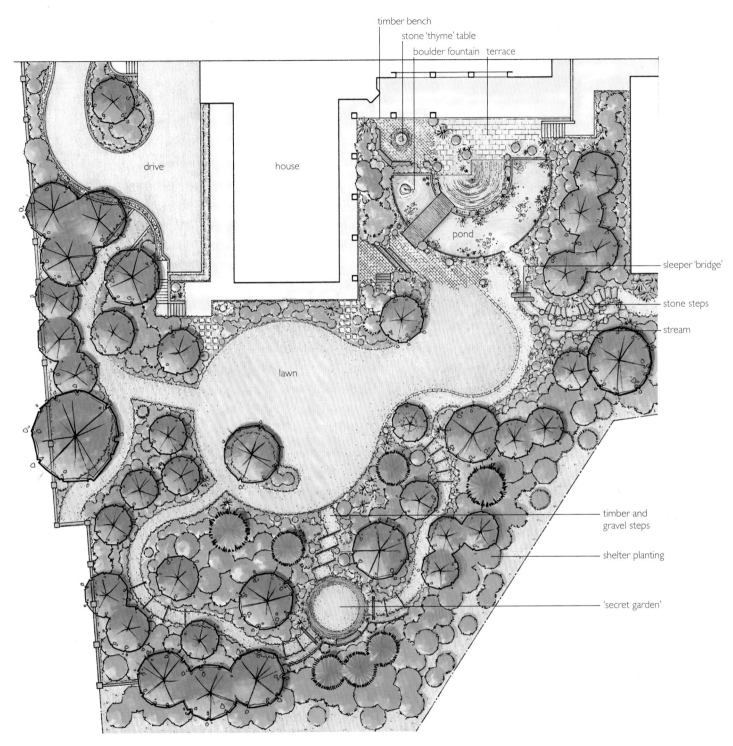

timber bench

stone 'thyme' table

boulder fountain   terrace

drive

house

pond

sleeper 'bridge'

stone steps

stream

lawn

timber and
gravel steps

shelter planting

'secret garden'

through it during dry spells. This is a very sinuous garden created from interacting circles and winding grass alleys and gravel paths, set against an exceptionally angular house.

It was a brave move to introduce circles into an environment mandated by straight lines, but this has been done ingeniously. All the hard landscaping materials have been restricted to the areas where family pursuits occur. These become more relaxed the further from the house you go, with grass and gravel taking precedence. Natural materials such as wood and sandstone and a twisting stream all combine to make a harmonious, almost invisible join with the panorama beyond.

A geometric semicircular pool edged with engineering bricks picks up the fabric of the house. The fountainhead for the pool is created from a drilled boulder. A wooden bridge spans its width, connecting the steps leading from the house to the barbecue terrace with its custom-made timber bench on the far side.

LEFT AND BELOW: *A natural stream feeds the main pond. Wild planting creates a lush, rich feel. The strappy leaves of phormiums, iris and daylilies are a bolder version of the grasses around the pond.*

manner. Picture windows and glass doors look out at all levels onto the commanding view of the countryside in the distance. A series of pre-existing steps lead down to a terraced level which had to be incorporated within the design.

The site itself was difficult due to its exposure to the southwesterly winds and noise from a very busy road. The garden therefore needed to be wrapped around by tree and shrub planting to afford some protection and to provide the desired tranquillity. In addition, they had to contend with a heavy clay soil which tends towards waterlogging in winter and wet summers, and becomes concrete hard with great fissures running

A waterfall splashing over sandstone rocks runs parallel to a flight of stone steps. A wooden bridge made of two railway sleepers spans the stream.

Textures are all important, with light-coloured, almost white setts and slabs specified for the entire terraced area. In many instances these have been laid horizontally to add further dynamism and rhythm to what could be large impersonal areas. The very pale colour reflects the light and provides a definite contrast to the darker stones and boulders that soften the edges of the pool.

Plants have been selected to show their architectural forms. Each tries to echo the next, setting up a natural pulse through the garden. Soft grasses, *Miscanthus sinensis* 'Gracillimus' and *M. s.* 'Zebrinus', with their gently arching leaves and downy flowers, mirror the strong shapes and colours of *Phormium tenax* Purpureum and *P. t.* 'Yellow Wave'. The pond and streamside have become a riot of textures and soft colours, all picking up the sunlight as the breeze blows through them. They look so natural one could almost believe they have arrived by chance.

The geometric shape of the pool provides an interesting counterpoint to the stream and waterfall that feeds it. These are bounded on one side by dense shrubbery and on the other by a gravel path which resembles a beach. Another crossing point over the stream has been constructed using two railway sleepers which have been angled to create an informal bridge. The large sandstone rock bank which retains the tree and shrub border also hides the source of the stream, which spills down over the rocks beside the stone steps.

The gravel path meanders through the garden, gently moving from one evocative area to another, carefully feeding the senses with yet further surprises. It continues past a meadow towards a lookout point at the apex so that the countryside comes right into the garden. Turn round and paths lead off past plantings of *Betula pendula*, *Pinus uncinata* and *Prunus triloba* 'Ukon' and *P. cerasifera* 'Nigra', with tantalizing glimpses of the formal lawns beyond.

RIGHT: *The fields beyond the boundary exert a major influence on the garden. Where the stream runs its course, the plants have been chosen to blend into the landscape.*

BELOW: *A consolidated gravel path leads to a rustic wooden bench hidden in a thicket of hemerocallis, miscanthus,* Alchemilla Mollis *and fargesia.*

A garden should feel natural. The design should not be imposed on the landscape, rather it should almost be invisible, evoking the feeling that 'it's always been here'. This is easier when the house is old and constructed from local materials. Add mature trees and the fields of the Sussex Wealds coming right up to the boundary, and any garden designer with soul should be able to create a really special place. With the added bonus of a stream running the length of the garden, a designer should be in his or her element. But too often our interpretation of the site sends us off course. It's old, it's traditional, and the client hankers after roses round the door and the chocolate box image of a country garden. All tall lupins and hollyhocks.

Nothing could be further from this execution supplied by Acres Wild. This garden demonstrates their affinity with nature and their ability to allow the greater landscape to be encompassed by the garden. They have not compromised their strict adherence to strong architectural lines and simplicity. In fact, they have turned the hard landscaping on its axis so that it now lies diagonally

RIGHT: *A silver-leafed willow contrasts with the mature weeping willow, while slender grasses and daylilies provide a complementary texture.*

across the garden. But, as always, it is their interaction with nature which is their strength; the hard landscaping is kept to a minimum while the emphasis is placed on soft, naturalistic planting.

Ian and Debbie have absorbed the spirit of this place and allowed it to dictate how the plan should evolve. The fields are now a natural extension as the rough grass meets the meadow planting and mown lawns within the garden. The meadow areas have been allowed to grow wild, with grass paths cutting swathes through them. The stream has been widened in two places to create vantage points from the gravel and grass banks. Consolidated gravel has been used to make paths and terraces, and the mellow colour complements the York stone slabs used for the terraces. Drought-loving species have been placed through the gravel and slabs to add to the wild feel of the plants.

A deliberately limited range of plants and colours was used to blend more sympathetically with the surrounding countryside. The native common alder, *Alnus glutinosa*, is a small bushy tree that bears bright yellow catkins in spring. It has been planted alongside the paperbark maple, *Acer griseum*, with its cinnamon-coloured bark and glorious autumn colours, and the curious contorted willow *Salix matsudana* 'Tortuosa', all of which thrive on the heavy clay soil. Masses of grasses and predominantly golden-flowered perennials are grouped to resemble broad brush strokes on a canvas. The wonderful true blue from *Geranium* 'Johnson's Blue' and the deep pink reflexed flowers of *Hemerocallis* 'Pink Damask' provide a foil to the many yellows.

LEFT: Miscanthus sinensis *'Zebrinus' with its yellow and green striped foliage provides a textural contrast to the dead flower heads of* Stachys byzantina *with its soft downy silver leaves.*

Flanked by tall grasses and rushes, a path of gravel and sunken railway sleepers leads to a gazebo situated at the point where gravel meets grass. Wooden benches provide sanctuary for visitors and staff alike.

During the past decade many large companies relocated, some moving into the countryside. This not only created a happier, healthier and less polluted working environment for the employees, it also saved the shareholders' money. Enlightened companies realized that offices alone were not the only solution, and that their employees' state of mind would be enhanced if the grounds were landscaped.

London & Edinburgh Insurance was one such company. When they relocated to Worthing, in Sussex, they approached Acres Wild to develop a wildlife garden that would be educational as well as serve as a recreational facility for their staff. It was particularly farsighted of them to invite the local community to enjoy this wonderful resource. The gardens are adjacent to the modern low-rise offices and the original lodge house constructed from Sussex brick and knapped flints. They are reached from a very busy main road, so they had to provide sufficient room for parking within the grounds, without letting it become intrusive. The soil is free draining and slightly alkaline which enabled them to use native plants mixed with the occasional cultivated perennial.

A nectar border surrounds the Training Centre where staff can relax in a small courtyard and absorb the heady atmosphere. Pathways lead past pools and ditches, on through wild flower meadows to hazel coppices and orchards. Again, a restricted use of natural materials and a limited number of plant species demonstrate perfectly that simplicity wins outright.

Towering oaks, *Quercus robur*, which live to a great age, native birches, *Betula pendula*, and wild cherries, *Prunus avium*, one of our most beautiful native trees, form the basis of the woodland. These have been underplanted with hazels and wild roses – dog and eglantine evocative of Shakespearian plays – and dogwoods, hollies, buddleias and goat willows. They provide colour and berries throughout the changing seasons and entice wildlife to inhabit the woods. To create a mood which would affect the people who use the space positively, Debbie and Ian have laid down a bold structural plan with softness introduced by means of the planting. Without this clear-cut geometry the garden would not hold up, but would quickly grow into a great unkempt mass and lose its sense of purpose.

RIGHT: Sedum *'Herbstfreude'*
('Autumn Joy') with the grasses
Carex pendula *and* Miscanthus
sinensis *'Gracillimus', provide*
both a haven and nectar for insects
and wildlife.

BELOW: *Wild flowers and tall*
grasses have been allowed to grow
naturally at the edge of the
woodland. A narrow grass verge
to the gravel path is kept trimmed
to show a clear demarcation
between the wild and the
controlled areas.

Set on a wild and windy hill, this sloping garden on the Sussex South Downs is directly exposed to the elements, but it also has a view of the village below and the Norman church with its simple square tower and clay tiled roof. This garden truly reflects the appropriateness of the site as well as revealing its 'genius loci'.

Not the most propitious of sites, this east-facing chalk slope is vulnerable to the salt-laden winds blown in from the sea. Nevertheless, by building on their knowledge of the plants and materials which can withstand this harsh climate, Acres Wild were able to develop a garden in complete empathy with its surroundings. Sheltered viewing points have been carefully introduced to allow the owners to sit out of the wind and drink in the atmosphere of the garden.

Natural materials have been borrowed from the seaside. Old timbers form the steps to the long pathway that leads down to a gate at the very end of the site. Focal points sit at an axis to the paths and under the trees. Hard landscaping is at a minimum. Only sympathetic materials have been used: natural stone and

ABOVE LEFT: *The reclaimed timber steps and wooden posts, with their swagged rope rails, continue the coastal theme.*

LEFT: *In this sun trap, a chunky wooden bench is surrounded by mounds of santolina, lavender and acid-green euphorbias.*

chippings, clay bricks and tiles, giant timbers for steps and retaining walls, decks and benches. Jute ropes slung from pillar to pillar form novel safety railings around the gazebo.

The gazebo itself has been modelled on the church tower, mirroring the square pointed roof and tiles. It has been carefully positioned not to look down through the garden. Instead it gazes across a flowering lawn which is mown regularly and a summer meadow which is left long to provide a textural contrast. For protection, the gazebo has been tucked into a shelter belt of mature and new trees. Native British varieties that will be successful on chalk have been used, *Taxus baccata* 'Fastigiata', *Carpinus betulus* 'Fastigiata' and *Sorbus aria*. Sea buckthorn, *Hippophae rhamnoides*, and *Euonymus japonicus* are so hardy that they will tolerate almost any condition, and have been used in

The gazebo, modelled on the local church tower, commands an open and uninterruped view to the English Channel.

massed clumps to form shelter since tender plants would not survive for long. The garden has become a canvas formed by great sweeps of silvers, greys and blues of plants that will actually flourish in this location.

Debbie and Ian are more than landscape architects, they are real environmental artists. Through their immense knowledge of the site and the suitability of the flora to attract fauna, they are able to bring about the most beautiful transformations. They understand the need for a garden to stand in its own right and, equally importantly, for it to impact on the landscape in a way which will work when it is viewed from the outside.

CHAPTER SEVEN

Moods

Bold, imaginative blocks of planting
create a powerful impact

ANTHONY PAUL

A derelict valley garden with silted pools and a brook prone to
flooding was landscape architect Anthony Paul's challenge
when he moved to the Black and White Cottage in 1977. Streams,
weirs and pools had to be reclaimed and the garden redefined for
Anthony to allow his passion for dramatic planting to take form.
His is no return to Jekyllesque style.

Although this predominantly green garden covers several acres,
it appears as an intimate enclosed space hidden within a woodland.
The design has enhanced the pools and streams, and introduced
views and secret enclosures that show works from the Hannah
Peschar Sculpture Gallery to best effect. Grass plateaux viewed
across stretches of still water provide areas for cool contemplation.

Anthony's passion for foliage plants and the repeated use of
the same plants in massive drifts unifies the whole. Huge blocks
of *Gunnera manicata* with their enormous dark green palmate
leaves are offset by the ten-foot high white starry flower spheres
of *Heracleum mantegazzianum*. Dinner-plate leaves of *Darmera
peltata* and petasites edge the pools. *Pontederia lanceolata* in simple
dark blue-glazed pots adorn the decking terraces and also feature
in the stream beds. In springtime they are juxtaposed against the
delicate plantings of snakeshead fritillaries and species narcissus
in the grasslands.

LEFT, ABOVE RIGHT AND RIGHT: *The gardens surrounding the cottage
are formed along the Standon Brook, where bold blocks of architectural
water-marginal plants now flourish.*

Anthony is a flamboyant designer with a love of big spaces. In his landscapes the outside blends naturally with the man-made inside so that you cannot see the join. He is never happier than when he has to work with a huge backdrop such as the Swiss Alps and lakes or the Australian outback.

Anthony's enthusiasm for using natural materials, whether it is timber or stone, runs like a theme through all his designs. Outstanding plantings with the judicious placement of modern sculptures also demonstrate his flair for the unusual. Colour is another important factor in his work. Primary colours through to subtle stains guide the eye.

This hillside garden has majestic views towards Lake Lucerne and could easily be overwhelmed by the Alps in the distance, but Anthony has cleverly created a garden at one with its environment. Utilizing existing terraces from an earlier age, paved areas, steps and pathways have been created from large blocks of granite and local stone. Wonderful patterns have been woven into the design using smaller cobbles and setts. These

ABOVE: *The sunken circular pond is the pivotal point of the waterways where rills meet, circulating the water round the garden. Soft rounded stoneware pots commissioned from Chris Lewis add a touch of femininity.*

RIGHT: *'Spires', a specially commissioned sculpture in Welsh slate created by German artist Herta Keller, stands on a secluded grass terrace.*

often act as a directional change, as with the sunken circular pool. Stone rills carry moving water throughout the garden.

The dramatic level changes, flowing water and grand scale allowed Anthony to plant with his usual boldness. His love of water plants and his trademark use of vivid swathes of one plant variety, is seen to perfection. Within the sunken pool garden, *Alchemilla mollis* and other self-seeded plants have been encouraged to grow through the paving cracks. The fresh lime colours complement the tall spikes of *Verbascum olympicum* and the soft pinky-mauves and woolly silver leaves of *Stachys grandiflora*.

Although the climate is severe, the rills are abundantly planted with many favourites: *Iris ensata, Zantedeschia aethiopica*,

The jewel-like colours of Iris ensata, Lythrum salicaria *and* Verbascum olympicum *surround the sunken pool.*

Ligularia 'The Rocket' and *Hosta sieboldiana*, with their blue, yellow and white hues, sit happily alongside pink-flowered geraniums and purple loosestrife to blend naturally with the environment.

His preference is to use structural and large-leafed plants to achieve both form and volume. Nevertheless he does not dismiss the more whimsical foliage plants such as *Crambe cordifolia* as these provide a perfect foil to his emphatic statements. These lighter notes in his planting seem to let air into the design and help link the garden with the elements.

has its place. It has been planted up to look as natural as possible, blending into the background rather than competing with it. The ambience reminds me of the Kashmiri Mughal gardens leading down to the edge of Lake Dal.

Anthony is a freethinker with a very naturalistic style and a strong sense of direction and structure. His use of natural materials makes them look as though they arrived by the hand of nature, but their placement is absolutely precise.

Slabs of granite lead down to the swimming and rock pools which are bisected by decking. The soft greys of the timber and stone reflect the hues of the distant lake and mountains. A series of giant granite stepping stones set among the water lilies appear to float across the rock pool. In the furthest corner Anthony has placed a vertical sculpture surrounded by verdant planting: a red-leafed acer, its lacy leaves tumbling over the water source, with mass planting of *Macleaya microcarpa* in the background.

Water is a major influence on Anthony's designs. A garden above Lake Lucerne capitalizes on the link between the garden and the wider landscape, demonstrating a perfect transition from the tamed to the wild. A flat expanse of water is bounded by a shaped wooden deck on the near side, with a dense planting of iris, *Pontederia lanceolata* and grasses on the far side. A humped wooden bridge spans a stream that appears to disappear into the distance. The Alps rise mistily far away and blend with the sky.

The proportions of this garden are in perfect scale with the environment. The garden itself is an intimate area held within the clasp of a much wider horizon. Standing on the edge of the garden, one feels at one with the landscape.

Anthony's particular quality is to design a garden on the grander scale without being intimidated by it. The block planting is powerful, with only a limited number of varieties so that each

ABOVE & LEFT: *The bridge links the water to the lake. The early morning sun makes the vibrant colours of the irises and grasses appear translucent.*

RIGHT: *Large stone slabs appear to float across the water garden past a modern sculpture by Irish artist Noel Scullion, linking the garden to Lake Lucerne.*

Wherever physically possible, Anthony designs with water. Many water-loving plants have huge leaves which suit his theatrical style superbly. Colossal leaf structures form exciting pictures and bind a site together. The visual effect of water reflecting the leaf shapes adds a unique dimension to any garden. An additional joy of bringing water into play in a garden is its attraction for wildlife.

The wooded Surrey countryside dropping away from the poolside provides the backdrop for this garden. A very different atmosphere from the Swiss Alps, here Anthony has created a feeling of space within an enclosure.

Colour plays a crucial role in this water garden. Simple decking stained a vivid blue leads down to and around the pool, providing a superb contrast with the vibrant yellows of the centaureas, *Centaurea macrocephala*, and clashing pink heads of the foxgloves.

Square decking stepping stones stride across the pool, giving access to the far side and the vista across to woodland.

The water acts as a mirror and reflects not only the sunlight but also the surrounding planting. Without this large expanse of reflected light, the garden might appear gloomy and be absorbed into the background. Instead it has cleverly brought the wood into the garden without dominating it.

Striking architectural plants, mainly herbaceous, have been used to create a seemingly overgrown, jungly wild appearance, effectively linking it with the tree canopy beyond. Classical acanthus, bear's breeches, with its handsome glossy leaves and unusual mauve and white flower spikes, and the large yellowy-green flower heads of *Euphorbia characias* subsp. *wulfenii*, are in startling contrast to the bright yellow of the centaureas and the

pink of the foxgloves. Massed planting of *Petasites hybridus* with its huge rounded leaves, one of Anthony's favourite plants, can be seen across the pool. This is a water-marginal plant that can reach over three feet high and carries numerous pink flower heads. Tall clumps of grasses reflect the sunlight through their leaves, mixing with graceful *Iris sibirica*, the deep yellow spires of ligularia and the blue-leafed *Hosta sieboldiana*. The stately *Aruncus sylvestris* provides a feathery note in the background.

Here again, Anthony has concentrated on a small number of plants to keep patterns and textures to a complementary few, allowing the eye to rest and take in the entire scene.

BELOW AND RIGHT: *Blue decking unites the bog garden and woodland. Mass planting of* Petasites hybridus *takes on fiery tones in autumn.*

and tranquillity, using many of the Far Eastern works of art Michael has collected on his travels. These have been set to great effect within the planting. Again relatively few species of plants have been used, and those chosen have been carefully selected for their leaf form, texture or shape. Green and its many shades predominate. Giant blue-leafed hostas provide the perfect foil for the lacy leaves of *Acer palmatum*, the purple-leafed variety, and *Matteuccia struthiopteris*, the ostrich feather fern. The small-leafed invasive creeping plant mind-your-own-business, *Soleirolia soleirolii*, has been allowed to self-seed between the flagstones, adding a lush green and creating the appearance of moss.

The whole garden is one large pool, with a serpentine path of York slabs leading the way through river-washed cobbles from the

ABOVE: *Curved granite kerbstones span the tranquil pond. A small stone terrace serves as an al fresco dining room.*

RIGHT: *A bamboo bird scarer pours water onto two stones set at the water's edge. Sweetly-scented plants help to enhance the mood.*

In the hands of an inexperienced designer, taking elements from the Orient and incorporating them in garden designs outside their native lands can sometimes appear quite bizarre. Using a spattering of artifacts and adding the odd rock and Japanese acer does not necessarily make a good combination. Empathy with the site, scale, simplicity, good structure and texture are the criteria for creating oriental garden style. By adapting Zen principles to suit our needs, we can create an atmosphere reminiscent to that of the Orient. Anthony has created beautiful intimate gardens based on Zen teachings, borrowing freely from their style and modifying it. He has also been able to use his favourite elements: water, strong shapes and textures.

For his twin brother Michael, a well-traveled photographer, Anthony has created a garden with an amazing sense of peace

A decking terrace is raised above a dry gravel garden planted with clumps of the blue-leafed grass Festuca glauca, *bamboos and bright* Crocosmia *'Lucifer'. The blue furniture is reflected by the mass planting of* Agapanthus Headbourne Hybrids.

house to a York stone terrace at the far end. The pool is particularly beautiful. Lilies float on the still water at the far end, while a discreet fountain creates a whirlpool effect at the other.

In contrast to his brother's garden this dry gravel garden has a tiered decking terrace stained a very pale grey. The effect is almost monochromatic. This is Anthony at his most severe.

Timber decking is another material that he often uses in his designs. A natural yet very versatile material, it can be cut to practically any shape and coloured to suit the individual garden. Timber also combines well with almost any planting scheme and site. Anthony is renowned for using flamboyant colours in his gardens and normally wood is no exception, so it comes as quite a surprise to find this pastel shade in such a hot courtyard.

Here the openness and light colours used for the timber, raised planter and pool create a very different mood to the enclosed green room of Michael Paul's garden. The brightness of the sun throws the shadows of the plants across the ground, creating patterns that in turn become part of the design. The rough, almost circular stepping stones snake through washed pea shingle towards the semi-circular raised pool. Gone is the lush planting, replaced by spiky leafed plants: a group of yuccas, clusters of blue grass and clumps of bamboo growing through the shingle. A massed planting of blue agapanthus fills the raised planter, adding a bank of cool colour. Typically, he has introduced a shock of colour, the fiery red of *Crocosmia* 'Lucifer' which brings vibrant life into what might otherwise be an austere garden.

walls to all sides of the garden. It is always important for Anthony to be able to mix textures to deceive the eye. In this instance square slabs of slate, laid horizontally with an avenue of terracotta pots filled with clipped box balls, act as sentinels. Visually these add width to the narrow entrance. Then one steps under the wisteria, now trained over an arch, into the paved terrace below. The eye isn't allowed to stop at the rear boundary wall, but is taken beyond by trickery. A centrally placed treillage archway frames an open trompe l'oeil doorway, with a view of Italy beyond. One is immediately drawn into the magic.

The great weight of the fig tree is supported on classical columns, while terracotta pots filled with exotic plants add touches of warmth. Slabs of rectangular York stone form the lower terrace, their joints unmortared. Violets, *Viola odorata*, and mind-your-own-business appear to fill every nook and cranny. This is heightened by Anthony's choice of extravagant planting. The fig itself has strongly sculptural lines, so only plants that enhance this mainstay have been used. Exciting specimens like the sago palm, *Cycas revoluta*, and the tree fern, *Dicksonia antarctica*,

ABOVE AND RIGHT: *Theatricality is the mood behind this Italianate garden both at night and by day.*

Whether in the city or country, Anthony has a way of bringing the unexpected into his gardens. Town gardens can be problematic. They lack rural vistas and are often small and overlooked. Anthony's designs are very much at ease with these constraints; the smaller the garden, the more theatrical his design.

On the positive side, city gardens have microclimates of their own that allow for experiments with more tender plants. This means that Anthony is in his element, and no more so than in this Italianate garden. He found a gnarled old fig tree and a 75 year old wisteria, a change of level, a south-facing aspect, and

LEFT: *An aerial view shows the grey-stained deck stepping up to the pergola. The seating area is planted with the large-leafed* Vitis coignetiae.

BELOW: *Soft foliaged ferns and acers act as perfect foils to the large-leafed hostas and strap-shaped leaves of cordylines.*

with its frond-like leaves, jostle alongside the architectural leaves of a banana plant, *Ensete ventricosum*, and the rice paper plant, *Tetrapanax papyrifer*. Several of Anthony's long-standing favourites have also been brought in to add colour and form to some of the darker corners. The tall yellow spikes of *Ligularia* 'The Rocket', *Alchemilla mollis*, mixed ferns and *Hosta sieboldiana* all interweave with the bolder plants. Bright pots filled with cerise busy lizzies and the orange and fire reds from clivias and canna lilies add splashes of intense colour.

Two further dimensions play important roles in this courtyard garden. The music created by the fountain helps cool it on hot summer days, while in the evening the golden light of candles casts beautiful shadows, creating an intimate enclosed space.

Neither limited space nor shade confound Anthony. In a contemporary town garden, he brings lightness by introducing pale coloured decking stepping up in blocks, while simultaneously creating the illusion of greater depth. This is enhanced by the solid square pergola covered by the wonderful *Vitis coignetiae* with its saucer-shaped leaves which provides a darker room-like area in which to sit. *Dryopteris filix-mas*, *Acer palmatum dissectum* 'Atropurpureum' and hostas mix with the spikes of cordylines to achieve a verdant planting. For once water has been omitted, but the senses are still tantalised by the sweet fragrance coming from *Pittosporum tobira*, *Trachelospermum jasminoides* and honeysuckle. The most unusual feature, though, is the use of reed panels to disguise the fences, bringing a tropical feel into this town garden.

LEFT: *A trompe l'oeil archway set in a diamond-shaped trellis shows a Tuscan landscape beyond. Large terracotta pots contain a selection of architectural plants, while the clipped box balls add permanent structure to the garden.*

RIGHT: *Cushions add bright splashes of colour. An oversized ogee pergola stretches the width of the garden over the triangular patterned paving.*

Anthony's love of travel and his experiences abroad influence the way he approaches his projects. This courtyard garden has been cleverly extended by the use of trompe l'oeil on the rear wall which draws the eye into the Tuscan hillside beyond. The trompe l'oeil is reflected by the wall-mounted arch, infilled with terracotta tiles and a wall mask.

It is the paving in this small space which is so detailed and unusual. Formed from a series of triangles stretching widthwise across the garden, each triangle is bordered by ribbons of dark slate. The textures and colours repeat themselves down the garden: first reclaimed York stone, then the warm jewel colours of African slate, and finally river-washed Scottish pebbles. A huge metal pergola stretches across the width of the garden, while a diamond-shaped trellis fixed to the walls reflects the slate squares. The planting is minimalist, but very architectural. Terracotta pots contain wonderful sculptural plants such as the Chusan palm, *Trachycarpus fortunei*, and loquat, *Eriobotrya japonica*, both of which will thrive in a sheltered garden. The strict regimen of clipped box balls is juxtaposed with huge hosta leaves and the tall spikes of lilies. The table and chairs are placed under the pergola canopy, the cushions adding the only splash of vivid colour to the garden.

A tiny backyard with its southern influences and geometric lines is similar in style to the courtyard garden. Pale colour-washed walls with diamond-patterned treillage pick up the shape and colour of the paving. A small blue and terracotta tiled pool shows off the fountain to perfection. North African overtones are palpable. Terracotta plinths carrying simple terracotta 'eggpot' containers are the same warm tones as the rendering to the base of the pool, evoking the warmth of a Tunisian evening. Lush planting comes from the gigantic leaves of a banana plant, *Ensete ventricosum*, next to a bird of paradise, *Strelitzia reginae*, with its smaller but no less dramatic spear-shaped leaves. Hardier plants such as *Magnolia grandiflora* and the feathery, fragrant mimosa, *Acacia dealbata*, add height and stability to this small oasis.

ABOVE AND RIGHT: *The cool colours of the trellis and furniture contrast with the warm terracottas of the pots, pillars and tiles.*

LEFT: *Natural wooden steps lead up to a decked dining area flanked by pots overflowing with the blue daisy-flowered* Brachyscome iberidifolia. *Edging the steps are pots filled with giant agapanthus showing their china blue flowerheads.*

RIGHT: *Architectural plants shape an intimate seating area with a huge blue-flowered hydrangea providing a long-lasting splash of colour. The unpainted wooden table and chairs blend harmoniously with the deck.*

All of Anthony's hallmarks are present in this garden of abundance in Jersey. Although this is a small town garden, it merges with the background to conjure up the feeling of an intimate space within a larger garden. Set on a slope leading up and away from the house, platforms built from different materials create distinct changes in texture. Gravel and paviors lead up to the timber steps which rise to a natural timber-decking platform. This becomes an outside dining room enclosed by outrageously luxuriant planting.

The textural pattern of the planting is evergreen in form and structure. The combination of the strong strappy leaves of *Phormium tenax* with *Fatsia japonica*'s glossy palm-shaped leaves contrasts with the smaller, fussier foliage plants which cascade down the slope and carpet the banks. The bright green of a hypericum nestling into a rosemary is underplanted with the glossy green small-leafed *Ceanothus thyrsiflorus* 'Repens' whose bright blue flowers are such a joy in late spring. This colour is echoed throughout the garden from the huge hydrangea that dominates the top terrace to the spherical flower heads of giant agapanthus. Pots on the steps and decking are filled with another of Anthony's favourites, the plantain lily, but this time a green-leafed variety. Tall spikes of variegated iris leaves mirror the phormium, while daisy flower heads and repeated colours help create a rhythm within the space. And of course there is drama, in this case from the only splashes of bright colour provided by the hot orange of Turk's cap lilies.

Right: *Stepping stones thread their way through a dry gravel bed which incorporates reclaimed railway sleepers laid across the garden.* Lavandula stoechas *softens the vista.*

Below: *The large clumps of catmint (nepeta) create a haze of blue, while the massed planting of thymes, pinks and lamb's tongue (stachys) adds varying shades of pink.*

How typical of Anthony to turn our preconception of his design technique on its head. Here a York stone path appears to run lengthways, intersecting the sleepers which run across the width of the garden. Even the planting is very different, with few bold-leafed architectural plants, simply soft pinks, mauves and silvers growing through the gravel beds between the sleepers.

But look carefully and you will see the hallmark of an Anthony Paul garden. A tall conifer hedge divides the garden from the house with a glimpse of blue trellis above. Steps lead down through the hedge into the dry garden where a clump of silver birches meets a grassed area. The gravel acts as a perfect mulch for the massed planting of *Lavandula stoechas*, sisyrinchiums, stachys and thyme. A seating area is placed under a purple-leafed prunus, while in the distance there is a bright blue pergola with matching furniture. A patch of sunshine is created by the golden hop, *Humulus lupulus* 'Aureus', scrambling over the pergola which

RIGHT: *An old stone watering trough forms the central feature of this courtyard garden. Pots filled with culinary and fragrant herbs mix with permanent planting.*

BELOW: *All the senses are teased. Bright blue spires of delphiniums and pale yellow verbascums add a vertical dimension while lilies, jasmines and roses release heady scents.*

links the garden to the wooded area beyond. Structural plants can still be seen throughout the garden. Tall spires of verbascum are echoed by the soft silvery-grey stachys flower spikes, while large clumps of catmint (nepeta) with their silver foliage form a haze of blue flowers, reflecting the colour of the pergola and trellis.

In this graveled courtyard garden, the focal point is an old farm drinking trough. It makes a magnificent raised formal lily pond surrounded by herb-filled terracotta pots. This is a hot scented garden filled with sun-loving species: deep blue delphiniums, verbascums, shocking pink cistus, and a *Crambe cordifolia*. The heady scents of jasmine, roses, herbs and lilies fill the air.

In his gardens Anthony uses huge drifts of a single plant or colour to transform the most mundane space. If we are not frightened of using materials on the grand scale and overcome our awe of them, Anthony Paul's bold plantings demonstrate how we can achieve stunning results.

CHAPTER EIGHT

Rhythm

An artist's passion for plants woven
into the broader landscape

DAN PEARSON

LEFT AND ABOVE: *In the 1996 Chelsea show garden the warm rich colours of grasses and herbs form an interesting textural pattern, while galvanized steel planters contain multiple-stemmed silver birch trees.*

Whenever someone speaks of 'a sense of place' in connection with gardens, I immediately associate it with Dan Pearson, a designer with an innate feel for the intangible quality of a site. Dan seems to be able to absorb the atmosphere and pull something very special out of the air. He has a unique ability to create the most beautiful compositions from ephemeral perennials. These are not dainty portraits in flowers, but bold statements arising from massed plantings of one species intermingled with a few select others.

Dan's passion for plants and gardens began at the age of five. At first it developed into an obsession for individual plants and the process of combining them together. Encouraged to experiment by his parents, his intellectual talents rapidly matured, but a technical grounding was essential if he was to go further. Landscape architecture was too limited as plants were his primary passion and he needed to understand them to enable him to work with space and hard landscaping. Courses at Wisley, the headquarters of the Royal Horticultural Society, The Edinburgh Botanic Gardens and The Royal Botanic Gardens at Kew provided him with the plant knowledge that he was seeking. Study trips to the Himalayas and Israel opened his eyes to natural and native planting. Nature then became his guiding light. He found his mantra for his future designs which are very much plant led. His plantings are now on the grand scale. Hundreds of the same plant are set in great sweeps which create a flow of colour at ease with the environment. These are akin to broad brushstrokes on an artist's canvas.

In 1996 Dan was awarded a Gold Medal for his fourth garden at the Chelsea Flower Show, 'A London Roof Garden for the Nineties'. This was a wonderful collection of wind-tolerant plants clustered in rounded 'hummocks' formed by soft scented herbs in tones of grey and silver, bronze and brown and contrasting bright green. So that we are not lulled into a false sense of security, Dan shocks us by adding bright, clashing red. As in nature, taller species are interspersed throughout the planting. Verbascums with their textured glaucous leaves and the brown prickly heads of the teasel *Dipsacus sylvestris* pick up the exact colour of the delicate grasses and fennel leaves.

Huge circular galvanized steel planters are filled with individual silver birches. The unusual combination of fescue grass *Festuca* with its wire-thin leaves and hardy pink-flowered thrift, *Armeria maritima*, is used for the underplanting. Roof gardens are notoriously severe climatically and few plants prosper or survive for long, but they do provide a really good environment in which to experiment with plant associations.

LEFT: *Within this community garden Dan was responsible for the planting. He has the ability to create movement within his gardens by his use of colour and texture. A cleverly placed wooden bench guides the eye towards an enormous water wheel which is just visible over a sea of flower heads.*

BELOW: *Recycled rusting oil drums spill over with the hot vibrant clashing colours of deep orange double-flowered cosmos, purple petunias and the permanent dark red leaves of a phormium.*

Today the local residents have taken over the running of their community garden. Even the pavements have become an extension of it, with huge brown earthenware pots and herbs packed into planting pockets at the base of the telegraph poles.

Public places within our cities have been neglected for too many years. Urban sites have been left derelict or paved over, with a desultory children's play area tucked away in a corner. Happily in recent years some open-minded people have begun to make these spaces more accessible and congenial. Admittedly London has more green open spaces and parks than the average city. These have been enjoyed by the public for centuries, but they are not usually intimate spaces where the local community takes responsibility for their upkeep. Now progressive residents of many squares have taken on the challenge to turn a dreary site into a wonderful garden. The horticulturist and author Roger Phillips was one of the first to galvanize his neighbours into action to transform Eccleston Square in London's Victoria.

Another example is Bonnington Square, just round the corner from the Oval of cricket fame. This is an inner London area that was under threat of development. Local residents, including Dan, fought a battle to keep this one open space within the area.

Having won, they then worked hard to raise money and earn grants to transform this derelict wasteland into a community garden which would radically change the face of the square.

This is a dynamic space which spills out onto the pavement. Gone are the constraints associated with communal gardens. There is still grass, but not in the usual oblong block with straight paths skirting edges lined with sycamores and grubby shrubs. Instead here are curvaceous gravel paths which lead to secret corners sheltering tables and seats. Vast blocks of Dan's favourite perennials, shrubs and exotic plants shimmer in the breeze.

Architectural shrubs are pivotal to the structure of the garden. A great vibrancy of colour stems from Dan's passion for using strong, contrasting combinations. They reflect the multi-ethnic background of many of the residents. Bright purples and oranges, pinks and yellows, bring a great feeling of well-being. The garden has a natural exuberance which joyfully bubbles over, revealing the passions that gardens and gardening can engender.

As I mentioned in the chapter on John Brookes (see page 26), Dan was one the three designers asked to create a garden for BBC TV's 'Gardeners' World' programme. This small garden perfectly demonstrates his immense knowledge of plants and their natural habitat. It also illustrates his genius for turning the most mundane thing into something quite out of the ordinary. All three designers were given an identical plot of land with the same brief, but it was quite astonishing to see how different the interpretations were. John's garden was level except for the trees and shrubs, but both Bonita Bulaitis (see page 32) and Dan chose to add height. Dan enjoys orchestrating the mood by introducing movement through light and dark or by changes in texture. Colours, perfumes and the ambience of a site are also influences.

True to form, Dan's garden is intimate. At the entrance to the garden the visitor has no idea of the secret bounty beyond. There is a wooden bench with sturdy seats and a planting of black bamboo providing shade. A grey gravel pathway curves through the garden alongside miniature cliff faces designed to refer to the rolling landscape. At the end a natural free-form pool is bounded by a clump of birches. Reclaimed concrete slabs have been broken in two, with the rough textured edge on the outside. They have been laid as a dry stone wall using soil to make up the levels. The 'hill' has been mass planted with box to form soft, green pillows, the simplicity contrasting with informality elsewhere.

The garden is built around the different, contrasting textures of the soft and hard landscaping. Dan has used his favourite mix of perennials so that the colours change constantly throughout the seasons, from the bright fresh lime greens and dark greens of spring to a mixture of pinks and purples in summer and autumn.

The simplicity of the solid timber bench at the water's edge only emphasizes the intricate patterns and textures of the vegetation around it. Planting on a grand scale like this, using one plant in quantity, helps to establish a rhythm and to bring a wonderful detail like this into prominence.

LEFT: *Inauspicious concrete paving slabs have been transformed into a textural dry stone retaining wall bounding the dark grey gravel path.*

ABOVE: *The oversized wooden bench at the entrance to the garden is enclosed by a semicircle of black bamboo to provide shade and intimacy.*

*The carefully selected foliage
harmonizes with the bright
lime green flowers of spurge
at the edge of the natural pool
to bring a touch of sunshine
to a damp spring day.*

Dan's creativity comes naturally. A textile designer mother and an artist father probably explain how he developed his passion for bold blocks of colour set against startling combinations. He has replaced formality and rigid lines with informal wild plant groups which sweep through both his town and country gardens. His use of surprising combinations of plants sets him apart from other designers. His pure love of plants and understanding of their habitats allows him to experiment with them in places that other designers would shy away from. He has managed to cultivate a style which is very much his own. This has evolved over his years of travel and observing and absorbing different influences from very diverse cultures and habitats.

Dan has a relaxed style, and his gardens reflect the feeling of a meadow in them. Although he uses many native species, they are really composed of selected perennials that give the impression of wildness. There is a freedom that makes his finished gardens feel very familiar. There are no invisible barriers telling you to stay away, or not to walk on the grass. His fabulous colours are harmonious and yet yield startling surprises. Dan also uses his plants in unexpected ways. I always associate country gardens with his favourite perennials. I have used many of the same species at Shalford House in Sussex where they are liberally scattered through the herb and grass beds. However, I never thought to try them out in a small space like a town garden, let alone in a roof garden. But this is where Dan wields his sorcery. His immense background knowledge of plants allows him to experiment and learn which plants best suit the location.

Roofs are inhospitable places, and plants rarely thrive under such circumstances. Pollution, high winds and exposure to extreme weather conditions all combine to deter lesser plantsmen. But when you glimpse this rooftop oasis nestling among the chimney stacks, you would think that it is in an ideal position, rather than set amid the harsh realities of London's atmosphere. Plants need a tremendous amount of care and attention to look good, and they become tired very quickly. There is no remedy, just brutality – dead ones have to be pulled out and replaced.

There is just enough room to tuck a table and chairs into the womb-like massed planting on the roof.

A touch of humour is added with flames of orange red-hot pokers issuing forth near the chimney and a topiary bird nesting on the gable.

Because roofs are prone to such adverse conditions he prefers working at ground level. If anyone understands this, it is Dan. For a while he lived in an upstairs flat, where he was forced to create a roof garden for himself, and you can see he had tremendous fun doing it. If a designer can't experiment with his own garden, where else can he show his true sense of humour? This minute space has just enough room to sit and relax, but it is packed with an eclectic assortment of plants, pots and a table and chairs. Every inch of space is utilized. Timber decking forms a lightweight covering for the flat roof and wooden planters enable the plants to be raised above the 'ground' level. Even the parapet walls are inveigled into use.

All of Dan's best-loved plants like *Verbena bonariensis* and *Stipa tenuissima* seem to have found a space and sway gracefully in the wind. A multiplicity of grasses have been planted in galvanized buckets, while herbs enjoy the heat of the sun. The yellow-flowering broom forms a bright patch which echoes the flower heads of fennel, *Foeniculum vulgare*. Despite the exposed conditions, lavender flourishes alongside the golden and green thymes. Every inch of space seems to grow something, either in custom-made planters or in pots and tins. This amazing collection includes alstroemeria, a bright summer flowering perennial whose flowers range from pale cream tinged with pink through to yellow, orange and dark pink. But for me the pièce de résistance is the bird's nest perched on the gable with a topiary bird on top. A massed planting of flame orange and yellow red-hot pokers, *Kniphofia* hybrids, appear to flare out of the chimney.

Designers are frequently asked to create gardens within a public area for a specific purpose. Hospices, hospitals and gardens of rest often need a garden in which patients, relatives, friends and carers can lose themselves. Frequently a board or committee will dictate what they want, which is usually a traditional rose garden with a lawn and perhaps a fountain. Sometimes they are more visionary and allow the designer a certain freedom to arrive at the best solution. These gardens should not be gloomy places. They need to reflect the strong emotions felt by the users. At the same time they need to aid holistic healing and, if possible, to help lighten the mood with humour.

I have worked on similar gardens and have had to battle to keep to the original purpose of the design. All too often each therapeutic department tries to whittle away at the concept and turn it into something to suit its own needs. It then becomes a compromise that loses its purpose and identity. A place where the patients can grow their own seedlings all too frequently becomes too much for staff and patients alike, and then the garden becomes neglected. Nothing is worse than these sad apologies for

A bird's eye view of the seaside garden with its sculpted seashell and loose planting of stipa, arundinaria, Verbena bonariensis, Sedum *'Autumn Joy',* Acaena *'Copper Carpet',* Betula jacquemontii *and* Arbutus unedo.

gardens. Hospital gardens must have direction and a firm design. A children's garden should reflect their needs and be built specifically with them in mind, a therapy garden for stroke victims needs to be designed to suit their capabilities, and a therapeutic garden should help heal those in need of mental help.

Dan has managed to create just such a garden within the grounds of Worthing Hospital in Sussex on the south coast of England. This was a collaborative scheme with sculptor Peter Randall Page and Steve Geliot set up by the 'Art in Hospitals' project. Always ready to try new ideas, Dan has created a sheltered garden between two wings by using grasses and plants that can withstand the prevailing coastal winds. Two beautifully designed benches of scalloped driftwood are snugly protected by the grassy clumps and birches.

This well-used hospital garden
has a honey-coloured compacted
gravel path which winds past a
crafted wooden bench designed by
Steve Geliot. It leads towards a
giant sea shell sculpture by Peter
Randall Page which is set among
the waving grasses.

Dan was approached to join a team working on a project at Althorp, the home of the Spencer family in the Midlands. This was to bring about the sympathetic development of the Diana, Princess of Wales Memorial Museum and Garden. He was torn about whether to take on such an important commission, but after careful consideration he agreed to accept this highly emotive project. The development programme was to be considered holistically, each part being related to the other, the interior of the museum, the conversion of the buildings and the proposed walk.

Althorp is an old established estate with mature trees, rolling countryside and a working farm. It has the intrinsic feeling of historic houses and parks, a sense of heritage and mystique. Dan was fully aware of his responsibility to maintain this aura. Over the years the grounds have largely been allowed to look after themselves. The bones of the park are wonderful, but the overall feeling was austere and the scale so immense that it felt less than human. Many old and beautiful oaks had died or been felled, their branches cut back and the enormous trunks left where they had fallen to provide shelter and sanctuary for wildlife.

A redundant gate now provides access to the park. The walk from the car park is over a quarter of a mile, and the whole route will take the public over a one and a half mile walk. Old stable blocks and outhouses have been converted into the museum and visitor centre, but the entrance to these buildings needed to be re-oriented through an old pump-yard located to the rear. Dan's input mainly concerned the treatment of the grounds and gardens that ultimately lead visitors to view the place where Diana lies at rest, while linking it with the visitor centre. This has involved him in many discussions with the architects and other designers retained on the project. His solution was very much that 'less is more' and this required the opening of vistas and views and cleaning up the landscape generally.

There are many wonderful features that needed to be emphasized which had been lost by the accumulation of planting over the years. Dan's first priority was to design a natural flow for the visitors to follow. New paths had to be created, trees felled and overgrown shrubberies and rose borders ripped out. He has planted fifty new oaks in an avenue along the car park walk to replace those that had been lost. Land has been cut away and brambles, nettles and weeds grubbed out, while tree canopies have been raised to allow the light to filter through.

The entrance to the centre is divided into an area where people can sit and relax, and another which provides entry to the museum. Seven huge rustic benches six and a half yards long provide a resting place here. A futher seven on the same scale, but this time finely honed, gently shaped and sculpted, have been placed around the Round Oval. Steve Geliot, with whom Dan worked at Worthing Hospital, designed these seats to reflect the magnificent old tree trunks left lying within the grounds.

Dan's interpretation of this special memorial is one of pure understatement. There do not appear to be any dramatic changes to the landscape, but it has been cleared of unnecessary overgrown shrubberies to open views and lift the lines around the Oval to lighten the infrastructure. A sweep of velvety grass cuts a pathway through rougher meadows of English wild flowers. Over two and half thousand perennials have been used to create this distant vision of a meadow. The island has been planted with a hundred rambling white roses that bloom only once in a season, designed to be dramatic and ephemeral against the dark backdrop. The lake will be planted with a thousand white water lilies, reeds and flowering rushes. No unnecessary frills, just a simplicity that will reflect the very essence of the place.

The walk back is along a nut walk of copper and green hazel bushes, a delightful piebald effect that screens any views of the lake. Dan has created a landscape of contrasts as people move from one light area into a dark space and on into another bright one. The shadowy corridors of copper-leafed hazels looking out over the sunshine-filled grassy swards all help to create the atmosphere.

Dan is first and foremost an artist, and a gardener second. His empathy with colour, nature and plants is the basis of his trade while the site provides the inspiration for his canvas. There is only one Dan Pearson and, although we can abstract from his designs, we will never be able to capture his unique spirituality.

RIGHT: *Specially crafted wooden benches overlook the Round Oval towards the island where Diana, Princess of Wales is buried.*

CHAPTER NINE

Innovation

The contrived meets the natural landscape
with versatitlity and resourcefulness

SARAH EBERLE

Sarah Eberle became aware of her environment at a very early age. Born and bred in the country, and educated at the well-known progressive school, Dartington Hall in Devon, she was able to benefit from one of the first courses on the environment to encompass farming and ecology. Her love of the countryside evolved naturally into a career based around the landscape.

She is as happy carrying out a massive landscaping project for an industrial development as she is working on one for a small domestic garden. Being a true chameleon, she can adapt her style to suit the needs of both town and country locations. Her one stipulation is that she will only take on projects which are linked with the scenery surrounding the site and take account of the local ecology.

Working from her Hampshire base, Sarah's approach reflects her bias towards the countryside where she is able to connect her schemes with the environment around her.

ABOVE: *A modern walled potager is bounded by grass that has been allowed to grow long, while a wide mown path curves through the garden beyond.*

LEFT: *A modern cruciform raised lily pond is set centrally in a geometric setting of bricks and gravel within a mixed shrub and perennial border.*

FAR LEFT: *A dramatic* Euphorbia characias *subsp.* wulfenii *takes pride of place among the many greens and textures of the plants.*

117

Sarah has an instinctive comprehension of the interaction of the man-made and nature. At school she had been totally engrossed in the course on the environment, ecology and farming methods. At Thames Polytechnic in Hammersmith, London she followed a five year course on landscape architecture, but she struggled against the rigid conformity of the subject. By her own admission she was not an easy student, always questioning as they had encouraged her to do at Dartington Hall.

Sarah loved drawing freehand in pencil as this allowed a greater sense of artistry. She has an innate ability to visualize scale and proportion without the use of a scale rule, but this led her into trouble with the hierarchy. At times she doubted whether this would be an appropriate career for her until, fortunately, a work placement out of college showed her that landscape architecture is really all about technique. She particularly enjoyed her last year under the tuition of Tom Turner. She was urged to

diversify and this allowed her the liberty she needed. With his support and advice, she was encouraged to go out alone rather than work within the confines of a team.

Back home in Devon she found that financial restraints had almost totally curtailed landscape architectural development in the area, and so she turned her skills to the more intimate art of garden design. As a qualified landscape architect, at first Sarah found this rather embarrassing since, like so many in that profession, she looked on garden design as a somewhat backward step. She felt that after five years of training she had somehow let the side down, yet private commissions were coming in. Her first major project was to redesign a large garden centre which took eighteen months to complete. Since then she has grown in confidence and has become much more adventurous with her designs, and it isn't surprising that she has also become happier in her role as a garden designer.

In the Eurostar garden, a flight of gravel and stainless steel steps leads up to a terrace of resin-bonded buff gravel where a table and benches are set under a bright yellow canopy. Formal topiary and espaliered fruit trees are offset by informal planting of perennials, ferns and grasses.

A show garden really allows Sarah to stretch her imagination to the full. In 1997 she designed a garden to coincide with the first year of operation for Eurostar, the train link between Britain and France. This rail link between the two continents not only represents the very latest technology in rolling stock, it has also meant a distinct shift in attitude concerning the preferred way to travel. The garden Sarah designed was necessarily abstract as it had to incorporate minute details from the countries linked by the new train and use them symbolically within the garden.

Using her combined skills as a landscape architect and garden designer, Sarah has been able to create a representative Euro-garden. It reflects the national characteristics of these countries while still not losing sight of the fact that this exhibit has to stand alone as a garden. It is structured, ordered and contemporary. Rendered and painted walls suggest the streamlined train, but could just as easily serve as boundary walls

The bright steel rails running through the grass have been extended to create a gateway and link to the greater landscape beyond. A bed filled with yellow roses, lavender and delphiniums is representative of England.

to a domestic garden. The plant groups represent the individual countries. She has planted fruits and vines for France, massed bulbs from Holland, begonias and ericaceous shrubs for Belgium and trees to depict the forests of Germany, while roses and lavender stand for England.

The plants in this garden have been chosen for their textural contribution. Many are a neutral green punctuated by bright yellow and blue, the colours of Eurostar. Most exciting of all is Sarah's use of polished stainless steel rails to represent tracks which run through the hard landscaping materials, a buff resin, white gravel and lawn. They brilliantly unify the garden and its purpose, namely to represent a Euro-garden.

LEFT: *An informal shrub and perennial border bounding the terrace is filled with evergreen plants that will provide colour and textural contrasts throughout the year. The smaller forms of sisyrinchium echo the tall lance-shaped leaves of a phormium in the distance.*

RIGHT: *The lawn sweeps down to meet the informal border planted beside a path running along the river's edge. Simple arches covered by a single species of rose have been placed regularly along the walk.*

The informal border and arches sweep back towards the house bringing a unity to the garden and providing protection for a table and chairs placed under an existing tree.

Inspired by our tranquil green landscape, Sarah is able to manage an easy transition from the garden to the wider vista. She can sit for hours absorbed by shadows and the effect of light and dark on the changing dimensions and shapes of plants. It is her ability to observe that guides her designs. This naturalistic approach shapes her gardens. She extracts the essence and transfers it to many of her schemes. She feels that this is our way of connecting with the landscape, and that gardens are so important because they are often the only way many people can communicate with nature.

Today, Sarah's own style has developed to include the larger landscape. Her bigger gardens are very minimalist, allowing nature to dictate what happens within the boundaries. In some gardens she just tweaks an area here or there to be more in tune with the natural harmony of the setting. She will preserve an atmosphere or, where there is none, create one to achieve a special link with the surroundings. She considers it vitally important for the garden to be appropriate to the site.

Modern gardens can sit happily within the countryside, especially if they are minimalist, but the whole ambience will be lost if the planting is unsympathetic. As long as the scale, proportions, axis and sense of place are considered within a design, it should lie comfortably within the natural landscape. As a designer, Sarah sees herself as a facilitator who can achieve the transformation of which the client has dreamed.

Textures created by plant combinations are all important. A house border of evergreen shrubs mixed with hardy perennials, many of which are also evergreen, will provide structure and colour throughout the year. Green is the predominant colour, while flowers are incidental bonuses. These permanent schemes mirror the images conjured up in her moorside vigils, reflecting light and shade with great intensity. As she takes you further from the house towards the fields beyond, her planting style becomes softer. Again there are perennials and shrubs in tones of green, resembling the wild edges of the woodland and hedgerows, so that they blend in with the landscape beyond.

It is never too early to introduce children to gardens and the natural environment. Unfortunately, today many children have little or no access to the countryside, so they have no appreciation of the great adventures that can be found outdoors. I was lucky in that, wherever my parents lived, we had some form of garden and play space. Sarah, too, has been affected and influenced by her childhood experiences, and these can be seen in her work. To my mind Sarah was the ideal person for Fisher-Price to choose to create a children's garden for them at Hampton Court in 1998. She also has children of her own and so can appreciate what appeals to their young and developing minds.

This garden is dynamic and irregular, filled with structures that form the basis for climbing frames and creative play. It is designed specifically to stimulate a child's imagination, yet it manages to span the tremendous gap between a playground and an adult garden. This is a vibrant garden in two distinct parts, divided by a playhouse which only allows access to the wooded rear area to little people. The garden is filled with contrasts on a massive scale. On one side you have the brightly coloured garden

ABOVE LEFT: *Bright primary colours have been used to stimulate children's imagination, while simple daisy-headed flowers, red-hot pokers and bronze-coloured grasses introduce them to plants.*

LEFT: *The painted animals on the walls are hidden from immediate view by banks of grasses and bright flowers. The snake is used as a link between the different areas of the garden, while the head of a giraffe hides a secret water fountain.*

filled with wonderfully painted wild animals: a lion and tiger hidden in tall grasses, the giraffe with its head in the trees, the snake slithering through the framework and down one of the walls. On the other is a secret woodland garden filled with interesting plants, shrubs and rough grass.

All the plants were chosen for the specific purpose of encouraging children to experiment. These include a corkscrew hazel *Corylus avellana* 'Contorta', nicknamed Harry Lauder's Walking Stick with its curious twisted stems, a willow *Salix alba* 'Dart's Snake' with hollow stems that make useful whistles, and feathery flower heads for blowing into the wind. The hard

The brightly coloured flowers of fuchsias, potentillas, coreopsis, crocosmia, helenium and red-hot pokers stimulate a child's interest in the garden.

landscaped areas are made from a special mix of crushed glass sealed with an epoxy resin which forms a safe surface ideal for biking, roller skating and skateboarding.

Sarah feels that it is only in the last few years that she has built up a truly workable body of knowledge. "There is so much to learn and so many facets in landscape and garden design that you evolve and become hooked for life." Sarah has such an innate talent that her evolution is bound to be remarkable.

Theatre

The unexpected brings
drama and humour into the garden

PAUL COOPER

ABOVE AND RIGHT: *The surprisingly contemporary courtyard at Parnham House provides an interesting link between the historic house and the modern. Formal paving helps bridge the different periods.*

Garden design was not Paul Cooper's first love. It followed after a successful career in both the UK and America as a sculptor and environmental artist. When Paul moved back to Britain, he was commissioned to create sculptures within a landscape and gardens, and from there the transition to designing the entire garden was just a step away. He had very little plant knowledge but this did not hinder his new career. In fact, it may have helped because he was unconstrained by a horticultural background. At that time his position as a lecturer in Art and Design at the University of Lancaster and visiting Professor at the Maryland Institute of Art allowed him the freedom to indulge in lateral thinking and arrive at unique design solutions. He is always creative and his work is often on the edge of the acceptable.

Paul's early work was quite restrained. 'Two Circles and a Stone Bridge' was a superb piece of environmental art he created in Wales, a slate masterpiece which reflected his earlier career as a sculptor. Sadly, it was vandalized and demolished, but Paul is very pragmatic about this. He considers that there is a time and place for everything and nothing is permanent, including gardens. This is a refreshing and different attitude, especially since we garden designers usually hope to see our achievements lasting well into the far distant future.

The furniture maker John Makepeace asked Paul to create a very different garden within a courtyard of his historic home in Dorset. Parnham House is a traditional stone house with mullion windows. Paul has placed a single piece of sculptured stone in front of the house behind the majestic entrance gates. It is an abstract octahedron set in an oval terrace of square slabs. Thin slivers of stone transect the eight segments of the oval and the whole is held in position by a single row of engineering bricks. This turns the entrance into a stage set, and in this modern setting the existing plants in the shrubbery act as players.

To bridge the transition to the fabric of the ancient house, Paul has used a variety of natural materials in a more traditional way to help soften the effect. The remainder of the hard landscaping in the courtyard comprises rounded cobbles set in mortar and stone slabs placed on edge, together with random rectangular stone paths. Planting is totally incidental to the drama created by the simplicity of the single piece of sculpture.

Retro and modernism are not two words that I would normally associate with each other, but if an artist can turn a belief on its head, then Paul Cooper is the designer to do it. Taking a Thirties style house as his inspiration, he has created a minimalist garden to reflect its past. True to his tenets, plants have taken second place to the textures and contrasts of the hard landscaping. Strong geometric shapes on both vertical and horizontal planes, with stark white as the predominant colour, make this a very focussed garden. The exaggerated height of the pergola made of timber fencing posts directs the eye along a 'stream' towards a large concrete fountainhead that is the backdrop to the garden.

This is a multifaceted garden, and first impressions do not do justice to the intricate detail of the plan. If you look at a plan view of the garden, you see circles interlocking with a central path, but even the circles are not straightforward. One is partly grass, while a half moon of crushed gravel forms the other side which in turn becomes part of the path. The path itself is the intricate slate stream whose source flows down the centre of the panel at the rear of the garden. The path courses through a real pool, out through the paving, and weaves its way through shingle until it ends in a circular pool at the base of a pedestal fish fountain by Polly Ionides. Paul's play and interplay with the circle is totally absorbing.

LEFT: *The serpentine slate 'stream' curves down the path towards the pool at the base of the retro-style fountainhead. The base of the fountain has been silvered to reflect the water.*

RIGHT: *Oversized simple wooden beams have been painted white and deliberately left unadorned by plants in order to emphasize the simplicity of the design.*

Paul's off-the-wall zaniness comes out in his recent creations in the most unconventional ways. A typical Victorian terrace house gives the lie to what hides in a back yard built on two levels. In this truly extraordinary garden the occult meets the vicar. The top section has a traditional brick terrace with a bench and appears to be a typical English garden until you realize that the vicar taking tea is a perfectly painted cut-out, which happens to look remarkably like Paul. Minimal planting has been used, but those selected are exotic and architectural so that they form a green screen at the top of the retaining wall. This divides the lighter top level from the darker basement area.

LEFT: *Hades replicated in a suburban garden. The creative use of coloured lighting helps pick out the distinct levels and themes.*

LEFT AND ABOVE: *Special features adorn the garden. The cut-out figure of a vicar sits comfortably sipping tea, while a devil's mask is illuminated within the rock face.*

There is a slow dawning as you realize exactly what he has depicted: here we have hell in the nether regions and heaven on the upper level.

Rough hewn rocks enclose this small terrace. Nooks and crannies have been left so that little gems such as old bones and claws can be secreted away and ferns can take root. Lights hidden in other nooks provide a furnace-bright orange glow to accentuate some rather macabre relics and a metal devil's mask. An old animal skull has been used to make the strangest fountain.

The whole terrace is enveloped by a specially commissioned metal arbour which represents the planets orbiting the sky. To enhance the mood, special lighting effects have been installed to emphasize the atmosphere at night. There is a deep pink glow at the lower level, while a golden light shines on the vicar.

Nothing can be further removed from the typical cottage-style garden than this futuristic one. Here Paul faced a problem often found in suburban gardens. Small, dank and dark, the sun rarely gets in to warm it for it is permanently shaded by the tall conifers of neighbouring gardens. The client has a busy lifestyle and only has a chance to relax in the garden in the evenings. Paul looked on these challenges with relish as an opportunity to use his innate talent for the unusual. If the sun would not come into the garden, the garden would have to come up to meet the sun.

This is probably one of Paul's most thought-provoking gardens. White railings with a blue wavy line and metal steps take you up to unexpected heights, making it difficult to know whether you are on an ocean liner or in a factory. Neighbours used to conventional gardens with grass and roses must have been shocked at the transformation. With overtones taken from his Chelsea 'Hanging Gardens' exhibit, Paul has created a multilevel living area which utilizes both horizontal and vertical planes to the utmost. Based on precise geometric lines, the whole garden has been raised and decked. Each level can be reached either via a ladder or by metal steps which lead to metal and timber walkways. For safety reasons, narrow railings and metal mesh screens have been fixed to the raised walkways, but these are also geometric and fit harmoniously into the overall theme.

The garden is composed of a series of large planters made of metal and lightweight white board which reflect the light. They have been fixed at various levels to increase the overall planting area. A number of platforms have been included so that the garden can be viewed from all angles. This means that Paul's client can relax in the sun, which was quite impossible in the original garden.

The garden has also become a huge adventure for children. No ordinary garden could stir such interest or have so many secret spots, as well as different levels to explore. A totally safe rubber floor substitutes for a lawn, a great compromise as no grass would flourish in this space. Alternative surfaces such as stone,

Switching on the lights brings about a magical transformation.
Strategically placed uplighters help create a sense of theatre.

White painted railings with blue wave details and metal stairs link the various decks throughout the garden.

selection was to have plants which foam over the edge rather than trail over and smother the planters. Paul was mainly concerned with the plants' interaction with the night-time lighting. They had to be dramatic in shape since the interplay of light and shadow is an essential part of the design.

An inspirational element of the garden is the full height steel fountain, likened by *The Independent on Sunday* to a huge cheese grater. Water spills over waves of rippled, polished steel which refract the light, creating a dramatic focal point both in daylight and when the fountain is illuminated at night. The fountain has been strategically placed to hide a neighbour's thuggish conifer.

The garden may appear quite bizarre in daytime with its hard railings and hidden video, but it really comes into its own at night. The lighting has been placed so carefully that it turns into a futuristic outside room at the flick of a switch. Paul's pièce de résistance is a giant video screen created by the series of white boxes. Any film or show can be viewed at leisure from inside the house or out. Love it or hate it, it is pure theatre.

Paul's inimitable designs are quite apart from those of his contemporaries. He comes from a different discipline and does not get bogged down with garden lore and its folk heroes, and experiments with incongruous materials that often jar with conventional thinking. Who else would use gravel as a substitute for water in a fountain, or hang used tea bags from a shrub? One year Paul bemused us all by bringing a disused mine shaft overrun by wild planting back to life at the Chelsea Flower Show. He is not a comfortable designer as he is always pulling the unexpected out of the ether. Lateral thinking is brought to bear on many of his projects and as a result we benefit and learn from his amazing mix of discordant materials.

In today's hectic world, we are constantly on the move; houses change along with lifestyles, careers and even partners. Paul believes that gardens should reflect our contemporary culture and therefore should also be considered transient. This is open to debate, but certainly garden designers should not be

aggregates, decking or concrete are sometimes used in such situations, but I have rarely seen rubber, normally found in children's playgrounds, used in an area like this. This is a really versatile material as it is safe, can be moulded to virtually any shape and can be coloured to suit the needs of the garden.

Paul freely admits that he is not a plantsman, but his partner Jo Matthews is a horticulturist, so teamwork went into creating just the right uncluttered look. A low maintenance garden with year-round interest was essential for this non-gardening client. Jo experimented with plant associations and textures, with deep colours on the top layers, grading down to silvers, greys and whites at the lowest level. Fragrant evergreens with white flowers predominate, echoing the white planters. The logic behind the

looking inward. By their very nature, gardens are always changing from season to season. As there is an accepted shift in nature, so there is also room for innovation. Garden history has not stood still. Requirements have radically changed over the centuries and now we have reached a moment when natural resources are under threat. Paul, the sculptor, frequently works with stone and wood, but in his gardens he uses synthetic materials and disposables. Recycled products frequently find their way into his schemes along with many unconventional materials.

When Paul began his career in garden design, his plant knowledge was limited. This did not seem to matter as it was the hard landscaping with its many textures that was important in his early commissions. As his designs progress, it is noticeable

The view from the conservatory at dusk is like watching the lights go up on stage. This startling installation evokes a real sense of drama.

that the soft landscaping is taking on a more important role, necessarily interacting with the metals and stone. Perhaps over the years of working with plants they have begun to permeate his thoughts more? They add to the structure and texture of his designs and even they reflect the humour of the finished garden.

Paul is a stimulator. His thinking is so original that many cannot accept it as garden design. Others believe that his approach is the way ahead and that it is time that designers begin to look at alternative and creative ways in which to advance our work. Life would be very boring without his input.

CHAPTER ELEVEN

Order

Strong stucture and bold planting
within intimate settings

ANDREW WILSON

I first met Andrew Wilson in the late eighties when I was a raw student of garden design. Andrew was then a senior lecturer and is now the Principal of the Inchbald School of Garden Design in London. Through him I was able to overcome my nervousness of putting pen to paper. Both of us have never looked back.

Our paths cross frequently through the Society of Garden Designers or the Inchbald, and recently he installed a small terraced garden near me in Middlesex. This is an enclosed back yard in a conservation area near the River Thames. A working client like this one who travels frequently needs a garden which can be enjoyed at any time of the year, day or night.

A conservatory built on to the rear of the house has been paved with the same stone as the garden to give the illusion of greater space. A shallow level change adds further interest, while dynamics have been added by the inclusion of two narrow strips of contrasting stone running through the garden. These continue right up to the rear of the conservatory. Discreet uplighters which have been countersunk into these two slate channels make a terrific impact at night.

This is a very structured unit. The angular lines of textured natural stone slabs, cut into borders mulched with grey chippings, are offset by dark purpose-made trellis and treillage boxes set

LEFT, ABOVE RIGHT AND RIGHT: *A small garden really comes into its own when lighting is included in the design. The mood swings from a sunny courtyard to that of drama when the lights spotlight its features.*

intended to become an architect, but then turned to working with the landscape instead. It was during Andrew's successful career as a landscape architect that he collaborated with plantsman Peter Thirman on a project for British Rail at Lewes Station in East Sussex. Between them they created a sub-tropical scheme on part of a disused railway line which is reminiscent of the hothouses of Kew Gardens.

It was Peter who encouraged Andrew to take up lecturing and this led to his position at the Inchbald. A natural and enthusiastic communicator, Andrew has carved out a niche for himself. As a landscape architect, he admits that when he started at the School he really did not know very much about garden design. This was at a time when landscape architects were considered superior to garden designers. Nowadays, Andrew says that he feels privileged to be associated with a profession that is in the ascendancy, and he has come to regard himself as a garden designer first and a landscape architect second. He believes that garden design is an art which has something unique to offer and from which landscape architecture can learn a great deal.

Andrew sees his role as a problem solver in both his guises, on the grand scale as a landscape architect, and on a more intimate

against the walls – well-defined lines combined with exuberant planting. Many architectural plant shapes grow through the moisture-retentive chipping mulch. Andrew and his client were keen to preserve the one good feature of the garden, a gnarled old fig tree, and this now has a pivotal role within the design. The garden has also become a gallery for Andrew's client to show the artefacts she has collected on her travels.

Andrew is a landscape architect by training and is currently completing his doctorate in landscape design and environmental studies. Both as past Chair of the Society of Garden Designers and as an author, he has an influential role within the landscape and garden design fraternity. In his early years he loved being in his parents' garden, and gradually his interest in gardens, plants and urban spaces developed into a vocation. At school he developed his facility for design and painting. He originally level as a garden designer. He has gone full circle and returned to the gardens and plants he loves. Unfortunately, he is unable to design more than three gardens a year while he is studying for a doctorate, but those he is able to complete demonstrate his versatility in dealing with all manner of gardens.

Andrew considers that there is an important dichotomy between personal and public space. In the former an individual pays for the work, while in the latter it comes out of corporate or council coffers. This certainly affects the way one addresses a project, but his design concepts flow from one into the other and his design principles have not changed radically.

Below: *The toning colours of gravel, cobbles and stone slabs create a harmonious background for the architectural plants and pots filled with bright seasonal flowers.*

Above: *In this show garden the crystal-clear water of the stream shows the large rounded boulders and smaller cobbles off to perfection, while coloured grasses provide textural interest at the edge.*

Andrew has no heroes in the gardening world, although he has been greatly influenced by the work of Preben Jacobsen. When Andrew was introduced to Preben's work at university, he was impressed by how dramatically different it was to the usual run-of-the-mill landscape design that was on offer in the early 1980s. Architectural and simple, the structure was truly beautiful. Jacobsen's attention to detail was inspirational, even down to the last specially commissioned brick. Jacobsen is a subliminal designer who seeks to convey his message as simply as possible, a principle which has guided Andrew ever since. While not losing sight of the disciplines of architectural landscaping, he has been able to shed the more rigid constraints it laid on him and design

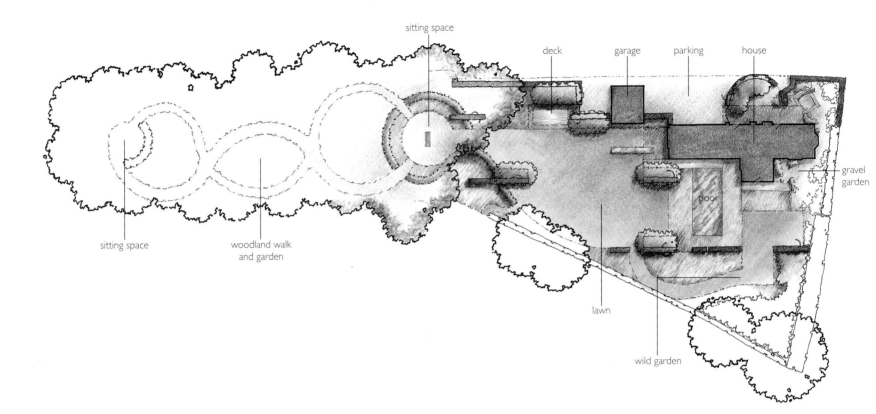

sitting space

deck   garage   parking   house

gravel garden

sitting space

woodland walk and garden

pool

lawn

wild garden

on a more intimate scale. Approaching a project as a garden designer, building on his love of plants and belief in simplicity, has given him new insight.

Combining textures and experimenting with new industrial materials within the domestic landscape has become all important to him. Using plants with architectural or light reflective qualities, a limited colour range, and a minimum of variegated foliage means that each leaf or plant shape has to correlate with the others to achieve the ideal result. Andrew is fascinated by the layers within a landscape. For him modern garden design is based primarily on verticals and horizontals softened by a layer of planting.

His approach to modern design is rather severe and can be almost surreal. He uses plants as sculptural entities grouped within the garden, either as solid blocks like clipped hedges to emphasize the horizontal lines, or as groupings of fastigiate trees to show the verticals.

It is rare in Britain for a client to have the confidence to give a designer an open brief. We always have to contend with the weight of our past. However, Andrew has one client who has the utmost trust in him and has given him carte blanche to develop his garden. This is a funnel-shaped area around an old house in Surrey which opens onto a neighbouring golf course and public footpath. This is home for a family with three children and two Great Danes, so the garden needs to provide space for them to romp and must also be able to withstand the rigours of family life. A new, uncompromisingly modern extension is being added to this traditional house, allowing Andrew to follow his heart and be just as resolute with his design.

The garden layout is still only at design stage. It has been simplified into a series of interlocking spaces unified by yew hedges of *Taxus* x *media* 'Hicksii', both within the garden structure and along the west boundary to increase privacy. These hedges are not intended to act as impenetrable boundaries, but more as

links between the different areas. They will also reduce the impact of the overall shape of the garden. This species of yew is columnar and makes an excellent hedge, and Andrew plans to have them well-clipped into slender hedges rather than allow them to grow into the robust ones seen at our stately homes. The hedges will be grown horizontally in line with the house. These very bold structural, almost sculptural shapes will emphasize the directional pull towards the natural woodland with its mown pathways and seating areas at the end of the garden.

Around the older part of the house Andrew has introduced a gravel garden with informal 'new perennial' planting mixed with ornamental grasses. This is a light and breezy area which contrasts with the elegant swimming pool garden tucked around the corner of one of the hedges. Here he has deliberately chosen to edge the pool with dark Welsh slate for dramatic effect, while the gunmetal grey used for the interior walls of the pool maximizes their reflective quality. The hedge beyond will have a

Views caught between the hedges beyond the swimming pool provide a glimpse of the dynamic and changing images of the garden beyond.

pencil-thin gap to allow a narrow corridor of light to be reflected on the dark surface of the pool.

Throughout the garden Andrew plans to have sculptural spiral lights in stainless steel. These will emerge from both sides of the hedges, with their supports hidden by the growth, so that they look as though they are unsupported. This will be a garden of many parts, but it will need time to develop before its full potential can be realized. This is a rare and extraordinarily far-sighted client who is willing to allow a design to be implemented which will take years for its real joys to be seen.

Andrew is a dynamic designer, always shifting at the boundaries of design, driving us towards a new dimension. He is a generous and inspirational teacher. All of us can learn from his simplification of design and from his minimalist techniques.

CHAPTER TWELVE

Space

The interaction of rhythm and moods
within the landscape

SALLY COURT

I have always been fascinated by the interplay of light and
shadow within a space. Light plays spatial tricks, deceiving us
into believing that objects are closer or further away than they
actually are. To deceive the eye, one designer will use trompe
l'oeil, while another will use the ruse of borrowing the greater
landscape and incorporating it into the garden. We are all great
hoaxers, and I am as bad as any. Not all designers are fortunate
enough to work on large projects. Many domestic gardens are
small suburban backyards where space is at a premium, so it is
extremely important that scale and proportion are faultless if the
garden is to look right.

As a designer, I put my soul into a design, and would be
unhappy if one of my creations was merely transient. I believe
gardens are long term, but all the same I appreciate that they are
constantly changing. That is what makes them so exciting, and as
long as the basic structure is solid, one can modify and update
the frills. I get a real thrill every time I revisit a site and find that
it has more than exceeded my expectations.

I have some clients in Sussex who are a joy to work for and
have put their utmost faith in me and my ability to interpret their
needs. Their garden is large enough for experimentation and I
have been given a free rein to try out planting schemes and
combinations that may or may not work the first time round.

*Looking across the stream-fed carp and lily pool towards the brick and
oak pergola, the eye is drawn to a pair of red-leafed acers.*

FAR LEFT & LEFT: *A mown grass path through the meadow alongside four huge 'grass beds' lead the eye towards the summer house which is set among specimen trees to form the beginnings of an arboreatum. During the winter the beds continue to provide colour and interest with great plumes of dried stems and seed heads.*

RIGHT: *A reclaimed York stone path cuts through the croquet lawn. Young clipped box are being trained at the edge of the steps and retaining wall. Graceful birches and a willow tree have been planted around the ornamental carp pond.*

Some time ago I was intrigued by speakers at a Kew symposium on modern German thinking on herbaceous borders, and my client subsequently visited Munich. As a result I decided to plant two 'grass beds' approximately fifteen yards long by five yards wide. They are set in front of a backdrop of mature beech trees and bounded by a wild flower meadow. The idea was to blend the rough meadow grasses with the taller ornamental grasses in the beds. Grass pathways bisect the beds and allow for easy access through the meadow, providing a continuation of a softer planting theme.

One of the joys of being a garden designer is that you are constantly bombarded with new ideas, materials and plants. When I drew up the original planting scheme, I imagined I was a bird flying over the plot, gently being carried by the wind. Some of the plants were clustered as though they had sprouted where the seeds had landed, while others were singletons, placed sporadically as though they had been dropped. It was a very informal method and proved to be very successful.

It was wonderful to see how well the original selection seemed to be doing a year later. *Alopecurus pratensis* 'Aureus', the golden fox-tailed grass with vivid gold and green stripes, nods heads with *Pennisetum alopecuroides* 'Hameln', a robust upright variety with amazing bottle-brush flower heads. Even more exciting is the mix of *Arundinaria viridistriata* with its rich yellow and bright green variegated stems, *Molinia caerulea arundinacea* 'Karl Foerster' with great plumes of golden brown arching flower spikes, the truly breathtaking *Imperata cylindrica* 'Red Baron' and the more delicate *Stipa tenuifolia*. These have really outshone their descriptions, towering gracefully in the beds and exceeding their height specifications.

I wanted the beds in the Sussex garden to be attractive throughout the year, so I included perennials among the grasses for added zest. Hemerocallis with its sword-shaped leaves and lovely coloured flowers, and *Eupatorium purpureum* 'Atropurpureum' with its dark stems and rose-purple flower heads, mix superbly with the grasses. For added colour the daisy-like flowers of *Coreopsis grandiflora* and *Rudbeckia maxima* sit happily alongside strappy-leafed kniphofia, while the tall plumed heads of *Macleaya microcarpa* wave in the late summer breezes. The flowers are reflected in the jewel-coloured heads of the *Leucanthemum* x *superbum* varieties and the *Echinacea purpurea* hybrids.

The beds have proved so successful that a further two have since been added. They seem to thrive on composted bark mulch and very little water. There is only one problem – the gardener finds it difficult to differentiate between unwelcome grass species and those we want to establish. The blend of the meadow and the grass beds has worked exceptionally well, creating a harmony between the areas and leading happily into the wilder areas surrounding the valley streams and pool.

The pool was originally buried in depths of dead bamboo, fallen trees and bracken, and was puddled out from a small dead overgrown pond. To make matters even more unsavoury, the outlet pipe from the ancient and cracked sewer led straight into the black water. Eventually a new sewage treatment plant was installed and nowadays the pond is crystal-clear and much increased in size. It is a very different scene which greets us. The banks have been planted up with a mix of native and cultivated plants. Duck houses and a floating platform provide safe havens from the foxes for ducks, coots and moorhens, though not from the increasing numbers of grass snakes. Where once there was silence, bird song is now constant. It is pure delight to know that many wild animals are coming back to this once barren spot.

The pool nestles in the junction of the wooded hillside and the meadows. Drought is not a problem as water from a large bog and springs continuously feeds the pond. The excess water, once

ABOVE: *In spring azaleas and the red leaves of cobnuts bring early colour.*
LEFT: *Drama is provided by the giant leaves of* Gunnera manicata.

directed through pipes to a lower level, now tumbles over a rocky waterfall set in a hollow in the broad-leafed woodland.

The wild garden extends over some fifteen acres, so it was necessary to create a walk to make much of it accessible. Paths and steps have been made from recycled chippings and logs from trees felled during the creation of the garden. Tracks lead through the woods and past the pond and clamber up the steep hills. It is awe-inspiring, so we have placed many seats where you can catch your breath and admire the view.

The natural beauty and sheer size of the horizon beyond the garden dominates the way it has been developed. The garden is a series of linked spaces that lead from one distinct area into

From the formal sunken herb garden, steps lead up to the pergola which is covered in whitebeam and fragrant white-flowering wisteria.

another. Each has a common theme to bring unity to the whole site, but each is necessarily different. There is a herb garden on a plateau just above the valley where the tree ferns, *Dicksonia antarctica*, *Gunnera manicata* and *Rheum palmatum* thrive. It will eventually be surrounded by an eight foot clipped conifer hedge which will provide shelter and privacy, and also hide the reclaimed railway sleepers that have been used for the retaining walls. This will be a secret enclosure within this very open garden. Raised beds are laid out formally, with an oblong pool

145

and a specially commissioned shell fountain by sculptor Fiona Barratt. Great banks of soft-coloured plants which give off heady scents fill the deep borders, creating a warm and sheltered spot.

I have designed this garden to be singular. Each part is unique and is often called by a descriptive name given by my contractor and friend, the poet Phil Dodson. The large terrace to the front of the garden is of reclaimed York stone rescued from a railway station that was undergoing modernization. This terrace and the croquet lawn are two of only five really flat areas in the garden. Planting here is a mix of modern herbaceous species and traditional clipped box. For fun and structure, I have planted eight standard evergreen strawberry trees, *Arbutus unedo,* on a level below the croquet lawn. Their wonderful ball-like heads come just above the terrace, so from the house you see a series of bold spheres hovering above the wall. From below they form a marshalled structure within the border, with great fountains of golden *Stipa gigantea* appearing like haloes above.

The house sits atop a hill looking down over a valley towards densely wooded hills in the far distance. It is an intimate property and the gardens need to reflect this. Although this is a traditional seventeenth century timber-framed house, the garden does not follow the typical cottage style planting. The view is spectacular and needed to be brought into the garden so that it can be seen clearly from the house terraces. Over 1500 overgrown conifers were felled to open up the view and allow a vista. New tree planting sympathetic to the site has taken precedence, along with the channelling of the many natural springs into a series of pools and streams that eventually connect with the pond in the valley.

The springs feed a large informal pool near the house spanned by a simple stone bridge. Water courses through two further pools planted with water lilies and marginals. It continues down into a stream which runs the length of the garden, and its planting has been modified to blend in as it travels through the different areas. The mood of the garden gradually becomes wilder as you move towards the valley and the woods.

Newly emerging foliage brings the first signs of the fresh colours of spring growth. Hostas and irises are among the earliest to show.

Even though space is at a premiumin in cities, people yearn for their own cultivated patch. Wherever possible they will find a small corner to create a garden they can nurture. This passion does not seem to be restricted to one nationality or country. This was very true when a client in the centre of London asked me to create a balcony garden for her. As with many apartment sites, this one was overlooked, so privacy was essential. Parking restrictions and weight constraints made delivering materials a nightmare, but I had a very enthusiastic client who had left a well-established garden in the country and was determined to transform this bleak balcony. I provided the basics – the creative ideas, the installation and the structural planting – and acted as a facilitator. My client was able to realize her passions and added the seasonal colour and frills that make this garden her own.

When building a roof garden you have to be careful not to trip over any hidden pitfalls. Before work begins structural engineers must supply the loading details. Local by-laws need to be thoroughly researched, and any management committee must be consulted and permissions obtained. Only when you are armed with all this can the planning and installation begin.

ABOVE: *A narrow passageway is decked with treated timber, while a border has been created from a single railway sleeper.*

This balcony provides a fire escape route for other residents, so a clear uncluttered pathway at least three feet wide has to run through it. Timber was my choice of material as it is so versatile and relatively lightweight. The balcony was narrow and the gate to the neighbouring terrace was located in an awkward corner, so to overcome this all the permanent beds had to be kept to the outside walls. I created planters at different heights to form a tiered system, with the deepest planting bed tucked into a corner at the rear. This enabled me to use trees in the scheme. The planters step down to two very shallow ones at the front to make a small pool and a herb garden.

FAR LEFT AND LEFT: *Cretan pots filled with bright plants add a vivid spot of colour, while a small shallow pool serves as an improvised bird bath.*

is not restricted to grass. The majority of plants have green leaves and provide a calming atmosphere if that is what one wants.

A small garden has many inherent difficulties: limited space, lack of privacy, poor views and unfavourable aspects. It also brings a great many benefits: cosiness and a perceived sense of protection, a unique microclimate and, best of all, it forces you to be more creative in your solutions. No matter how small or large, structure is all-important in a garden. I also believe that rhythms should be set up to bring about a natural flow through it. Whether by the repetition of a plant shape or texture or through the use of colour, this creates a balance so that a sense of place and mood prevails.

LEFT AND BELOW: *In spring the falling petals of the* Ceanothus *'A T Johnson' fill the unmortared paving joints with ribbons of blue. The architectural leaves of* Trachycarpus fortunei *rustle in the wind and fragrant flowered* Pittosporum tobira *spills over the small fish pond.*

My own garden is a thirty-by-fifteen foot terraced back yard on the outskirts of London, typical of so many found in this city. As a designer, I am torn as to the best way to deal with the juxtaposition of old and new. I am aware of the tremendous heritage we British designers have and I love using natural materials such as reclaimed stone and timber. Old clay bricks have a mellow look and seem to blend well with almost any planting, so I attempt to use them wherever appropriate.

But modern planting is something different. It can really change the dynamics of a garden and the smaller the plot, the bolder and more dramatic it should be. Forget the sweet peas, dahlias and begonias – they do nothing to enhance a town garden. Lawns in a small area are a menace and should be banned. Green is the most refreshing and soothing colour, but it

LEFT: *Pots in simple terracotta and coloured glazed finishes are clustered around the pool.*

RIGHT: *Three stacked trays of antique French clay pots with their repeating pattern make an unusual detail in the garden.*

As I have already mentioned, light plays an important role in all my work, and it is of particular importance in my own garden. Early in the morning, I am halted in my tracks watching the sunlight filter through the leaves of the birch *Betula jacquemontii* with its dazzling white stems, one of the most beautiful of the species that originates from Western Himalaya. In the evening, as the setting sun shifts, it highlights the feathery leaves of the acers near the pool.

The Orient and ancient Islamic paradise gardens have had a great influence on me throughout my career, and I have borrowed freely from their wisdoms to create my own paradises. Water is an essential ingredient. I feel that a garden without any water is incomplete. It need only be the tiniest feature; just a bird bath will do. Birds and other wild animals are another essential, and water encourages these delightful visitors to our gardens.

Dramatic leaves form a sense of the unreal. Palm trees in London? Why not? I even have parakeets dropping in. These escaped from their cages at Chiswick House during the storm of 1987 and have bred successfully in the wild, so they are not such an unusual sight hereabouts. Although at first glance my garden may seem lush and overgrown, in fact it is severely controlled. Colour themes run through it, plants are repeated and unwanted invaders ruthlessly weeded out. Many of the plants become too big for a small garden, so they are regularly cut back and shaped to ensure that the overall jungly feel does not get out of hand.

The Chusan palm, *Trachycarpus fortunei*, and its companion plants *Acer palmatum dissectum* 'Atropurpureum', *Pittosporum tobira* and phormiums are repeated throughout the garden, although not in the same colour combinations. One area has a concentration of red themes, another creams and greens which add balance to the other plants which have been brought in to complement them. A great canopy of blue flowers is supplied by the evergreen Californian lilac *Ceanothus* 'A T Johnson' that has been trained into a single stemmed tree rather than a dense bush.

This is very much a sensual garden, one where different scents tantalize at different times of the year. From the early flowering climber *Akebia quinata* in February, to *Trachelospermum jasminoides* in early summer and the potent *Pittosporum tobira* and pots of lilies in mid to late summer, all conspire to provide me with an excuse to linger outdoors.

An 'old cloister' was the setting for this medieval herb garden. Little details help place this garden in its period. The modern clay bricks are distressed and the joints are mortared with soil. The capital of an old column makes a fine stand for an armillary sphere, while clay pots are filled with herbs.

A friend involved me in a fund-raising event for The Royal Hospital for Neuro Disability in Putney in southwest London. This triggered off an emotive response in me, and I approached them with a proposal to see whether a show garden would help promote awareness of the Hospital. *The Mail on Sunday* generously offered to sponsor building the garden for the Hampton Court Palace Flower Show on the understanding that afterwards it would be rebuilt in the grounds of the Hospital.

The design had to reflect the very serious disabilities of the patients and their needs. It also had to sit comfortably within the grounds and the hotchpotch of buildings. Just as importantly, it also had to work within the artificial atmosphere of the Show. The design was loosely based on a medieval infirmary garden. All the materials are modern apart from the roofing tiles and the capital of an old column supporting the armillary sphere.

The oak cloister and pergola are constructed by traditional methods with all fixings doweled. The roof offers shelter for the large wheelchairs required by some of the patients and provides a seating area for visitors. The herbs were selected for their healing and soothing properties and many of them are scented. All encourage the bees, butterflies and other insects which joined us at the Show and later followed us to the garden's final resting place. This is truly a sensory garden.

BELOW LEFT: *Healing herbs fill the rectangular beds, while old apple species add height.*

ABOVE AND BELOW: *A basket of woven willow supports the living willow entry arch.*

The ultimate aim was to give the Hospital's patients, families and friends a garden in which to rest and contemplate, where they could forget their problems or come to terms with them. It was designed to be a therapeutic garden, not a therapy garden.

Many town gardens are at basement level and have to reach upwards. This can be problematic, as with this garden in Hammersmith, London. It is in a terrace of houses enclosed by high brick walls and has a fall towards the house. It backs on to a public park which is higher up than the garden. It is in a conservation area, so the local authority paid special attention and closely watched every step of the renovation.

Drainage was a particular problem. To prevent flooding, we had to drain the excess water from the lower level, so drainage gulleys and pipes taking the water to a soakaway under the terrace were installed. At the upper level we left the joints of the stone paving unmortared to allow the water to escape more easily. For security and privacy reasons, a brightly-stained trellis was fixed to the top of the walls.

In the park beyond, a mature canopy created by existing sixty-foot trees gives depth to this small garden. By linking shrubs and climbers to the natural backdrop, I was able to create the illusion of a much larger garden. My client had extensively modernized the interior of her four storey Victorian house, and a glass balcony at ground floor level leads out of her sitting room. Another small balcony outside the main bedroom also looks down on the garden, so that it is viewed from both above and below. It was therefore of paramount importance to create shape through structural planting and texture.

Sawn rectangular paving with gravel joints sweeps through the centre of the garden. Exotic architectural plants and soft foliage lead to the bench.

This is not a flower garden, but one of complementary leaf forms, and plants that do not die back in winter. They provide a tapestry of architectural plants with a single colour highlighted throughout the garden. The great strappy variegated leaves of the New Zealand flax *Phormiun tenax*, and *P. cookianum* in contrasting stripes of greens and reds, create a subtropical look, especially when mixed with the other exotics. In early spring, the deep red leaves of the delicate *Acer palmatum dissectum* 'Atropurpureum' start unfurling and match the warm colours of phormium.

Flowering plants are an added bonus, but they have only been used if their leaf shapes have a textural importance. A few, like *Magnolia grandiflora* with its large glossy green leaves and reddish-brown undersides, and fragrant creamy-white tulip-shaped flowers in summer, and *Clematis armandii* with clusters of scented flowers and leathery dark green leaves, found their way on their own merit. Water features are on both levels of the garden, and the sound of water playing is mesmerizing on warm summer days. Fountainheads in the form of a snake plaque and free-standing lizards, specially commissioned from sculptor Lucy Smith, make diverting details in this semi-tropical atmosphere.

LEFT AND RIGHT: *Water spills over the stone trough and is recirculated through an unusual fountainhead of two lizards, while a third sits on the wall above. Dwarf papyrus,* Cyperus isocladus, *flourishes in the mild London winter.*

The location is the real catalyst for stimulating a design solution. Clients of mine bought this property in Surrey purely for the sake of enjoying the view. The house is located on a hillside looking northwards over a superb wooded valley. The majority of the distant trees are broadleaf and turn the most magnificent colours in autumn. This is one of the most spectacular sights I have seen from a client's property. I needed to create a garden which would merge with the background while keeping its own identity.

Unfortunately, the site that went with the property was a nightmare. Set on the side of a steep hill, you needed to be a skilled climber to make a safe descent to the bottom which was also the sunniest spot in the garden. Therefore, the first task was to form a series of terraces and steps to make the garden usable. I worked with the contours to shape the garden which naturally divided into two parts. We levelled the area next to the house and laid it partially to lawn, and planted borders with shade-loving plants. A breakfast terrace was then laid at the edge of the fall into the lower half of the garden. This area is the link between the two halves. Three standing stones form a fountain that feeds a rill set in the stonework of the terrace. At the edge, the water from the rill tumbles over a waterfall into a holding pool at the bottom. The slopes have been densely planted with a multitude of irises, ferns, hostas and other marginal plants to form a cascade of early summer colour.

Shallow timber and gravel steps set into the hillside follow the contours round to a second terrace set at the very bottom of the garden which forms a perfect sun trap overlooking the pool and waterfall. The shrubs and trees for this level have all been chosen to either accent the colours of the woodland beyond or to provide a dramatic contrast. The choice of bold leaves and complementary colours repeated throughout the planting was essential to give structure to a garden that could otherwise have been assimilated too easily into the background and lost.

LEFT: *A wooden bench nestles under the canopy of an old yew tree, while the new planting of* Robinia pseudoacacia *'Frisia' provides a brilliant splash of colour from spring through to autumn. The leaves of* Paulownia tomentosa *can reach up to two feet across.*

ABOVE AND BELOW: *Standing stones sit at the head of the rill feeding the waterfall, while a flight of steps descends to the lower terrace. Phormiums either side of the path echo the shapes of the iris leaves mass planted around the waterfall.*

PLANT LIST

INDEX

ACKNOWLEDGEMENTS

Author's acknowledgements

I would especially like to thank the designers who feature in this book for giving their valuable time to take me through their experiences and the philosophies that are so unique to their styles. I am also grateful to the other designers who spared the time to share their thoughts. My thanks also go to the owners of the gardens who generously allowed me to use photographs of their special private spaces, and to the sponsors of all the show gardens illustrated in the hope that they will continue to support us as this is the only way we can promote excellence in contemporary design. To Tamar Karet, Pedro and Frances Prá-Lopez at Cardinal Publishing and Clare Churly at Ward Lock – thanks for your courage and faith. And for the advent of e-mail. Also to Betty, my mother who has been so unwell during the writing of this book, and my sister Alex for taking the load off my shoulders and for giving their unconditional love. And to Pepsi, Cola, Tom and Dick for their little escapades during this time that brought smiles to our faces, not forgetting David and Paul, Phil and Gary, as well as all my clients who have lived through this. And to all who have helped in the making of this very beautiful volume.

Picture acknowledgements

Photographs
Peter Baistow: 112-113
Malcolm Birkitt: 12-13, 32-33, 108 left, 109, 124-135, 142 right, 143, 144 top, 145-147, 150, 151 left
Christopher Bradley-Hole: 42
John Brookes: 6, 14-15, 17-23
Nicola Browne: 104-107, 110-111
Jonathan Buckley: 108 right
Bonita Bulaitis: 34-35
Sally Court: 144 bottom, 153 top
Bob Curtis: 28, 31, 36-37
Sarah Eberle: 119-123
Garden Picture Library:
  Juliet Greene: 118
  John Glover: 51 top, 52 bottom,
  Roger Hyam: 53,
  Michael Paul: 86, 103 top,
  J. S. Sira: 39, 60
  Ron Sutherland: 38, 88 top, 90-93, 94 top, 95, 96 bottom, 97, 98 bottom, 99-101, 102 bottom, 103 bottom
  Brigitte Thomas: 87 bottom

Steven Wooster: 16, 52 top, 87 top, 88 bottom, 89, 94 bottom, 96 top, 98 top, 102 top
Dr Bob Gibbons: 148-149, 151 right, 154-155
John Glover: 142 left
Jerry Harpur: 24-25
Andrew Lawson: 40-41, 56-57
Christopher Monaghan/Apertures Photographic: 7
Clive Nichols/Garden Pictures: 30, 34, 44-47, 140-141
John O'Brien/The Press Office Ltd: 115
Ian Pleeth: 73 top left and top right
Paul Reeve: 116-117
Derek St. Romaine: 62-69
Ian Smith, Acres Wild: 70-71, 73 bottom right, 74-85
Nicola Stocken-Tomkins: 152, 153 bottom left and bottom right
Julie Toll: 48-50, 51 bottom, 54-55, 58-59, 61
Andrew Wilson: 136-137
Peter Wilson: 156-157
Steve Wilson: 29

Garden plans and illustrations
Christopher Bradley-Hole: 43
Debbie Roberts and Ian Smith, Acres Wild: 72, 77, 80, 84
Andrew Wilson: 138-139